WAITING ON TABLES

WAITING ON TABLES

A Commentary on Acts 6 and 7

Richard H. Anderson

Foreword by Margaret Barker

RESOURCE *Publications* • Eugene, Oregon

WAITING ON TABLES
A Commentary on Acts 6 and 7

Copyright © 2022 Richard H. Anderson. All rights reserved. Except for brief quotations in critical publications or reviews, no part of this book may be reproduced in any manner without prior written permission from the publisher. Write: Permissions, Wipf and Stock Publishers, 199 W. 8th Ave., Suite 3, Eugene, OR 97401.

Resource Publications
An Imprint of Wipf and Stock Publishers
199 W. 8th Ave., Suite 3
Eugene, OR 97401

www.wipfandstock.com

PAPERBACK ISBN: 978-1-6667-3994-7
HARDCOVER ISBN: 978-1-6667-3995-4
EBOOK ISBN: 978-1-6667-3996-1

MAY 2, 2022 12:07 PM

Unless otherwise indicated, all Scripture quotations are taken from Scripture quotations marked (RSV) are taken from Revised Standard Version of the Bible, copyright © 1946, 1952, and 1971 National Council of the Churches of Christ in the United States of America. Used by permission. All rights reserved worldwide.

To my wife Anita,
This book is dedicated to the one I love.

Contents

Foreword by Margaret Barker | ix

Preface | xi

Introduction: Waiting on Tables: The Challenge | xiii

CHAPTER 1
　The Appointment of the Seven | 1

CHAPTER 2
　Stephen | 20

CHAPTER 3
　Accusation | 27

CHAPTER 4
　Abraham | 32

CHAPTER 5
　Joseph | 43

CHAPTER 6
　Moses | 48

Chapter 7
   The Temple | 69

Chapter 8
   End of Speech | 81

Chapter 9
   Reaction | 87

Chapter 10
   The Enigma of Acts 8:1 | 91

Chapter 11
   Burial | 97

Chapter 12
   Was Stephen a Samaritan? | 18

Chapter 13
   Conclusion | 110

Chapter 14
   Excursus: Criticism of the Apostles | 113

Bibliography | 117

Foreword

F AR less is known about the early days of Christianity than is usually assumed. The world of Jesus' followers in Jerusalem in the years immediately after his death and resurrection is still largely unknown. The few precious chapters in Acts raise more questions than they answer, and the popular picture is based on familiar assumptions. Examining the figure of Stephen and his speech in Acts 6-7, Richard Anderson asks some of these questions.

Who were the Hellenists and the Hebrews in the early community? Why did Luke call them 'Hebrews' and not 'Jews'? Anderson concentrates on Luke's careful use of words, many not found elsewhere in the New Testament, and thus adds detail to the rapidly changing picture of Christian origins. For some years scholars have been talking of 'Judaisms' to describe the diversity of religious faith and practice in the time of Jesus among the heirs of ancient Hebrew culture. Here we see the life and work of Stephen set within this complex society.

Anderson reminds his readers that Luke was writing for Theophilus the high priest, and that this speech must be understood in this context. He examines the speech, in detail noting allusions to scripture, and *which versions of the Scriptures* are used. From this he reconstructs the early Christian against the temple and its rulers. Their ancestors had murdered the prophets, but they had murdered the Righteous One. This was the theme of Peter's

Foreword

speech in Solomon's porch and of Jesus' parable of the tenants in the vineyard.

His conclusion about the identity of Stephen will probably come as a surprise, but the evidence to support the conclusion cannot now be ignored.

Margaret Barker
December 31st 2021.

Preface

I WRITE to acknowledge that the evidence about the Hebrews is not missing; it has been hidden. This book uncovers the hidden evidence.

Introduction

Waiting on Tables: The Challenge

Any time anyone writes a book about scripture, the first question asked is, "what have you to say that has not already been said?"

The thesis advanced that Stephen's speech shows Samaritan influence and that Stephen is a current or a former Samaritan, has overlooked significant facts. Furthermore, the argument in support of this radical claim has not been properly advanced.

Scholars have acknowledged that Acts 6:1 is an enigmatic verse. The account in Acts has obscured the conflict between the Hebrews and the Hellenists.

Ben Witherington III, The Acts of the Apostles, A Socio-Rhetorical Commentary (1968), 240, The material in 6:1-8:3 is some of the most complex and controverted in the whole book of Acts, and calls for careful discussion and detailed analysis.

Marion L. Soards, The Speeches in Acts, Their Content, Context and Concerns (1994), 58, The speech is the longest and perhaps most perplexing address in Acts.

Joseph B. Tyson, Images in Luke-Acts (1992), 111. In Acts 6:1-7 we are faced with the difficult exegetical problem of a controversy between Hebrews and Hellenists.

Introduction

Oskar Skarsaune, In the Shadow of the Temple, (2002), 152, says Acts 6 "is one of the most enigmatic and controversial passages in the New Testament."

Scharlemann, Scobie, Spiro and Wilcox all suggested that Stephen's speech was based on Samaritan influence. Luke does not implicitly tell us that Luke was a Hellenist or a Hebrew or a member of another ethnic group. Joseph A. Fitzmyer, in discussing the distinction of Hellenists and Hebrews and their composition, recognized that the "latter group must have included converts from the Am ha'ares, from the Essenes and from the Samaritans, even though none of the last three groups are mentioned in Acts."1

Earl Richard, Acts 6:1-8:4 perhaps was too critical about scholars making theories without first doing a careful literary examination of the problem.

I am very much interested in Chapter 6-8:5 of Acts and particularly interested in the ethnic identity of Stephen and the Hebrews.

Todd Penner in his book, In Praise of Christian Origins, on page 71 citing in footnote 28, 2 Macc 4:10, 13, suggests that Luke has given us no clues as to how he wants the reader to understand the identity of these two groups. In my opinion both the Hellenists and Hebrews are outsiders having been denied access to the Temple relying upon the followers of Jesus for food and assistance.

The scholars have substantial disagreement with Stephen's speech. The primary focus is the criticism of the temple, its construction, its leadership and criticism of the belief that the Temple is the dwelling place of God. There is also a debate about whether the views expressed are those of Luke or Stephen.

For these reasons I have written this book.

---

1. Semitic Background, 279.

Chapter 1

The Appointment of the Seven

Acts 6:1 Now in these days when the disciples[1] were increasing in number, the Hellenists murmured against the Hebrews because their widows were neglected[2] in the ministry of daily[3] distribution.

6:1 Ἐν δὲ ταῖς ἡμέραις ταύταις πληθυνόντων τῶν μαθητῶν ἐγένετο γογγυσμὸς τῶν Ἑλληνιστῶν πρὸς τοὺς Ἑβραίους ὅτι παρεθεωροῦντο ἐν τῇ διακονίᾳ τῇ καθημερινῇ αἱ χῆραι αὐτῶν

THE followers of the Jesus movement adopted terms such as "disciples" to identify the members of their new religious community, the ἐκκλησία as the "true" people of God.

Luke has more references to widows and women than the other evangelists. Shuman noted "A widow becomes a widow only if and when she has no one to support."[4]

---

1. G3101 μαθητῶν;.
2. G3865 παραθεωρέω LXX none; Moulton, Vocabulary, (hereinafter M & M); Acts 6:1.
3. G2522 καθημερινός LXX none; M & M, 312; Acts 6:1.
4. Shulam, *Jewish Roots of Acts*, 303.

The word Ἑλληνιστῶν occurs here for the first time in Greek literature.[5]

Scholars have acknowledged that Acts 6:1 is an enigmatic verse. The account in Acts has obscured the conflict between the Hebrews and the Hellenists. Who are the Hellenists and Hebrews and why was there a need for a "soup kitchen" in Jerusalem? These two questions are related. The real reason chapters 6 & 7 of Acts are so enigmatic is that the evidence is not missing; it has been hidden. James Baldwin has an interesting quote we should consider. "The purpose of art is to lay bare the questions which have been hidden by the answers."[6]

David Pao has provided a credible solution[7] for the apostles refusing to wait on tables and appointing 7 men to do so for them but they after being appointed act as preachers by continuing their own style of ministry. Pao says that the Gospel of Luke has a continuing theme of table fellowship ministry whereby the table setting provides the venue for a ministry to the outcasts and oppressed. The table fellowship ministry was a venue for teaching and preaching of Jesus by word and by example. In Judaism, teaching was a regular part of the meal setting for the family religious meals. This may explain the ability of the disciples of the Jesus community to remember the oral traditions they were taught at meals hosted by Jesus. This is illustrated by the meal that followed Jesus' resurrection appearance on the Emmaus Road (Lk 24:27, 30). Pao observed that in both Luke 5:29–31 (Lk 5:30 ἐγόγγυζον) and Acts 6:1–7 (Acts 6:1 γογγυσμός), "one finds the act of grumbling in the context of a meal."[8] He further explained "In both contexts, the issue of complaint focuses on whether the outcasts can be included in the table fellowship of Jesus and his disciples."[9] The same complaint is made when Jesus goes to eat at the house of Zacchaeus, another tax collector (Luke 19:7). Jesus often used the meal setting

---

5. Johnson, *Acts*, 105.
6. Baldwin, "Creative Process", 18–19.
7. Pao, "Waiters or Preachers", 131.
8. Pao, "Waiters or Preachers", 138.
9. Pao, "Waiters or Preachers", 138.

The Appointment of the Seven

as a teaching opportunity. The inclusion of the outcasts in the narrative material connected with the meal scenes is a note-worthy theme. Meals in the ancient world often function to consolidate the boundary of an existing community "since social boundaries are enforced most rigidly at table, eating together becomes a mark of solidarity across class lines."[10] Meal scenes in Luke were designed to break such boundaries. By participating in table fellowship with outcasts and sinners, the Lucan Jesus challenged the traditional boundaries of God's community. Moreover, in the case of Acts 6, Pao recognized that these widows are twice marginalized, as they are not only 'widows' but also widows of 'the Hellenists,' who are outsiders.[11] As Pao explained "The critical difference is, of course, that in Luke 5:29–31 the complaint centers on Jesus' act of inclusion, but in Acts 6:1–7 it centers on his disciples' act of exclusion. Jesus' statement in Luke 5:31 that his inclusive mission is to focus on the outcast becomes a critique of those who neglect the widows in Acts 6:1."[12] From this, Pao concluded "The Seven therefore are to continue the ministry of Jesus, who was accused of eating and drinking with 'tax collectors and sinners' (Luke 5:30; 7:34; 15:1)"[13] because waiting on tables provides "the setting where table fellowship with the outcasts and the oppressed becomes possible."[14]

These insights provide support for the idea that both the "Hellenists" Ἑλληνιστής and the "Hebrews" Ἑβραῖος are outcasts who have been excluded from the Temple.

We do not know the origin of the meal program that became the subject of Acts 6. But "Of prime importance, nonetheless, was the fact that poverty was apparently a significant problem in the *ekklesia* of Jerusalem."[15] "In addition, we may presuppose that the majority of the urban population was also poor."[16] But the question

---

10. Acts, *Interpretation series*, 43.
11. Pao, "Waiters or Preachers", 138.
12. Pao, "Waiters or Preachers", 138.
13. Pao, "Waiters or Preachers", 139.
14. Pao, "Waiters or Preachers", 139.
15. Stegemann, *Jesus Movement*, 219.
16. Stegemann, *Jesus Movement*, 51.

persists as to why the Hellenists and Hebrews were eating together. If the Hellenists and Hebrews were the new "outcasts" in the continuation of the table fellowship ministry, who might they be? Since the Temple and the synagogues provided assistance for their members, the Hellenists and Hebrews may have been excluded from the Temple and the synagogues and thus precluded from the assistance programs provided by them. "Thus, it must mean that already the Christians were cut off from Jewish charities and had to set up their own system of poor relief."[17]

The food distribution program described in Acts came into existence because certain groups of poor people had a need and the community of believers who followed Jesus fulfilled that need. What is interesting is that there was already a food distribution system in place to which Hebrews and Hellenists as Jews had access. However, we know that certain Jews were denied access to the Temple and thus did not have access to the Temple sponsored food distribution system.[18]

The Temple did exclude people. Any attempt to provide a complete list of excluded people or the rationale for exclusion, is beyond the scope of this discussion. This list based, in part on Jeremias, *Jerusalem in the Time of Jesus*, is representative of the types of exclusions: those who practice despised trades such as tax collectors; Israelites with slight blemish such as illegitimate descendants of priests, (such as mother not of pure descent); proselytes, God-fearers, eunuchs, Gentiles, bastards, foreigners, Samaritans, and Jews who had forsaken circumcision. In addition, people with physical disabilities (See generally Lev. 21:17–23) were also excluded from the Temple: the blind, lame and lepers.[19] All of these people were considered unclean. Doorkeepers were stationed at the gates of the LORD's temple to ensure that the unclean did not enter.[20]

---

17. Finger, *Widows and Meals*, 255.
18. Magness, *Stone and Dug*, 78.
19. Jeremias, *Jerusalem*, 317–344.
20. 2 Chron 23:19.

The Appointment of the Seven

While passing between Samaria and Galilee, the Lucan Jesus met and healed ten lepers. Jesus instructed them to go and show themselves to the priests. One of the ten realizing he had been healed turned back praising God with a loud voice. He was a Samaritan. Jesus then said: "Were not ten cleansed? Was no one found to return and give praise to the Lord except this foreigner?"[21]

Using the same information available to Conzelmann found in Lk. 17:11, Annette Weissenrieder located the spot, being described, in the Valley of Jezreel. Weissenrieder further demonstrated how climatic conditions of this area would cause many inhabitants to be afflicted with a skin condition probably erroneously diagnosed as leprosy.[22]

Luke used the Greek word ἀλλογενὴς for foreigner. This Greek word is not only a hapax in Lk. 17:18, it is also the very Greek word used "on the well-known 'keep out' signs on the inner barrier in the temple."[23] In identifying the Samaritan as a foreigner, Jesus reminded his audience that Samaritans are excluded from the Temple. Thus, we have recognized two groups who were excluded, Samaritans and foreigners, that may help us identify the two groups mentioned in Acts 6. But first we must look at the language Luke employs in Acts 6:1.

As noted in Acts 6:1 Luke introduces, the Ἑλληνιστής and the Ἑβραῖος, two groups who had issues resulting in complaints against Hebrews because the widows of the Hellenists were being neglected in the daily distribution of food. Bruce has said with respect to the word Ἑλληνιστῶν: "Its formation indicates its basic meaning to be 'one who affects Greek ways' (thus it would naturally refer to non-Greek, not to Greek)."[24] Using the sense of what Bruce has said allows us to explain that Luke with the word Ἑλληνιστῶν was referring to the fact that many Judeans, including many of the high priests, had become "Hellenists." They had adopted Greek

---

21. Luke 17:11–18.
22. Weissenrieder, *Images of illness*, 224.
23. Marshall, *Luke*, 652. Bruce, *Acts*, 449.
24. Bruce, Acts, 181.

ways and the Greek language. In fact, the Maccabean revolt was at first directed against Hellenized Jews.

"Since Ἑβραῖοι are here distinguished from Ἑλληνιστῶν the word presumably used not as a synonym for Ἰουδαῖοι but in a narrower sense, of those Jews who attended synagogues where the scriptures were read and the worship conducted in Hebrew."[25] As Shulman noted: "Luke's contrast 'Hebrews Ἑβραῖος' suggests, as John Chrysostrom already remarked (cf. Hom. On Acts 14), that the reference is Greek-speaking—in distinction to Hebrew-speaking–Jews."[26] Theissen identified the two marginal groups as follows: on the one hand by people who had moved from Galilee to settle in Jerusalem (like Peter and James, Gal 2:18f), and on the other by the Hellenists, i.e. by Greek-speaking diaspora Jews (Acts 6:1f; Mark 15:21).[27]

However, since Ἑβραῖοι are here distinguished from Ἑλληνισταί, we should consider the possibility that just like the Hellenists are not Greeks, the "Hebrews" are likewise not Judeans, yet in fact speak the Hebrew language. This would mean there are two groups of people in Jerusalem speaking Hebrew. One group would be the Judeans.

Although Ἰουδαῖος is usually translated as Jews, it is likely that in the first century Ἰουδαῖος was understood as Judeans. This shift of ethnonym from "Israelites" to "Jews" is made explicit in the Book of Esther (4th century BCE).[28] Esler concludes that "Judean" is the most appropriate term and translation for the Greek word Ἰουδαῖος.[29] Esler was particularly convinced to translate Ἰουδαῖος as "Judeans" by a passage from Josephus (War 2.43ff cf. Ant. 17.254), which describes that the multitude from Galilee, Idumea, Jericho and Perea, and "the people" from Judea itself came to Jerusalem in response to the actions of Sabinus, the Roman procurator of Syria, an event dated to 4 BCE. Esler argues that the "critical point in this

---

25. Bruce, Acts, 181. Luke actually says Ἑλληνιστῶν πρὸς τοὺς Ἑβραίους.
26. Shulam, Jewish Roots of Acts, 304.
27. Theissen, Sociology, 57.
28. Chouraqui, People and the Faith, 43.
29. Esler, Conflict and Identity in Romans, 63.

passage is that the existence of a segment of this people lived in Judea itself was irrelevant to the fact that those of its members who came to Jerusalem were Ἰουδαῖοί."[30] The *BDAG* (2000) also prefer the terms "Judean" and "Judeanism" instead of "Jews" and "Judaism."[31] Thus it is far more accurate to speak of these people as "Judeans." From Acts 9 to the end of the book, Ἰουδαῖοι usually mean Jews and not Judeans or Judahites since the context is the Diaspora.

In fact, in 2 Macc. 8:1 the Greek term Ἰουδαϊσμῷ is coined to counter Ἑλληνισμοῦ (Hellenism 2 Macc. 4:13) and ἀλλοφυλισμὸν (foreignness; 2 Macc. 4:13; 6:24). Thus, the term "Judeanism" was used as a self-definition to distinguish its participants from the Hellenistic culture. The author of the Second Book of Maccabees presented the conflict as a struggle between 'Judaism' and 'Hellenism.'"[32] In this struggle, some of the participants disputed the validity of ancestral laws. Antiochus IV abrogated laws pertaining to circumcision, Sabbath observance and the kosher regulations.[33]

Second Maccabees uses the designation "ancestral language" for Hebrew language in chapter 7 in verses 8, 21, 27 as well as 12:37 and 15:29. Hebrew was also the spoken language in this time period. The author of Second Maccabees "regarded the Hebrew language as a very important marker of Jewish identity."[34] In chapter 12 of the book of Jubilees, the angel tells Moses about Abraham learning Hebrew, the language of creation.[35] In a Qumran text, 4Q464 we see the first explicit reference to Hebrew as the "holy language."[36]

Dunn states: "The abrupt juxtaposition of the referents 'Hellenists' and 'Hebrews' is very telling. The word 'Hellenists' (*Hellenistes*) means 'one who uses the Greek language.' weight to the

30. Esler, *Conflict and Identity in Romans*, 67.
31. Danker, *A Greek-English Lexicon*, 478.
32. Boin, "Hellenistic Judaism", 167–96.
33. 2 Macc. 5–7.
34. Schorch, Pre-eminence Hebrew Language, 46.
35. Jub. 12:25–27.
36. Schorch, "Authority of Torah, 12.

fact that the two terms 'Hebrews' and 'Hellenists' are set in some contrast."[37] Yet Dunn is guilty of the same error.

Luke is a very careful writer with a very large vocabulary. "There are about 19,000 words in his Gospel and 971 of these are hapaxes; there are about 18,000 words in Acts and 943 are hapaxes. Thus, one word in twenty in the Lucan writings is a hapax."[38] Luke is credited with being the first author[39] to use the word Ἑλληνιστής which appears twice in Acts. He obviously wants his audience to understand his new word which he accomplishes by using it near the Greek word Ἑβραῖος which means one who uses the Hebrew language. Thus, his audience understands that the word Ἑλληνιστής in the present context must mean one who uses the Greek language.

However, it is generally agreed that most residents of Jerusalem spoke Aramaic. For instance,

> Is Luke making a linguistic or ethnic distinction? His practice elsewhere is illuminating. He uses the term "Hebrew" (*hebraios*) only here, but when he uses the adjective *hebrais* it is always to refer to the "Hebrew dialect," (Aramaic), in other words, as a linguistic category. In the present case, therefore, the "Hebrews" would naturally mean Jews who speak exclusively or mainly Aramaic.[40]

As Nehemiah, in an earlier time, observed "they did not care to speak *Yehudit*."[41] There can be little doubt that Hebrew was superseded by Aramaic as the commonly spoken language in Judah during the Persian era.[42] However, Hebrew continued to be the language of the cult and the language of literature—which were both religious. It was also used on coins, probably due to the economic influence of the temple.[43] We know based on findings

37. Dunn, *Beginning from Jerusalem,*, 246, fn 20.
38. Orton, *Synoptic Problem and Q*, 194.
39. Bruce, *Acts*, 181.
40. Johnson, *Acts*, 105.
41. Neh 13:24; Kottsieper, *did not speak Yehudit*, 95.
42. Kottsieper, *did not speak Yehudit*, 109.
43. Kottsieper, *did not speak Yehudit*, 110.

The Appointment of the Seven

from Masada that priests were the primary leaders behind the use of Hebrew.[44] The default conclusion became that the Ἑβραῖος are Aramaic speaking Jews living in Jerusalem. Joseph A. Fitzmyer, in discussing the distinction of Hellenists and Hebrews and their composition, recognized that the "latter group must have included converts from the ʽAm ha-ʼares, from the Essenes and from the Samaritans, even though none of the last three groups are mentioned in Acts."[45]

In Acts 6, Luke clearly intends the First Reader to understand "Hebrews" to be members of the community of the followers of Jesus who speak Hebrew but are not considered to be Judeans or Hellenists. The ministry of meals served two separate communities, neither of which were accepted by Judaism. The seeds of these advances had been planted earlier by the Lucan Jesus and the ministry of the seventy. How are we to resolve this problem with a solution that retains the use of the Hebrew language in this setting? There are several possible solutions:

1. Since Hebrew was spoken in the temple precincts and in at least one synagogue in Jerusalem, Luke is referring to current or former members of one or both of these groups;

2. since in the Hasmonaean era a large body of Hebrew literature was created, of which the Dead Sea Scrolls constitute the largest remnant, Luke is referring to former members of this group now residing in Jerusalem; and/or

3. the Samaritans who spoke Hebrew and called themselves Hebrews from the third century B.C.E. [Ant. XI viii 6] but in the first century Jews did not call themselves Hebrews.

It is important to first recognize that there is no mention of the Jews or Judeans in Acts 6 or 7. The RSV does not use the word 'Judean' but 'Judean' appears 22 times in the NRSV including once in Luke-Acts in Lk. 1:39 translated from the Greek. Therefore, we can conclude that the dispute between the Hebrews and

---

44. Kottsieper, *did not speak Yehudit*, 115.
45. Fitzmyer, *Semitic Background NT*, 279.

the Hellenists did not include the Judeans. We can further state based upon this verse: "But the LORD said to him, 'Go, for he is a chosen instrument of mine to carry my name before the Gentiles and kings and the sons of Israel; . . . .'"[46] that Luke did not consider the Samaritans to be Jewish. In short, most Judeans were no longer communicating in Hebrew and thus would not be included in the group identified as "Hebrews" by the author of Acts 6. Consequently, it is probable that Luke is referring to Hebrew speaking Samaritans[47] now residing in Jerusalem. The conflict also concerned the right of the existence of the two groups within the community.[48]

None of the scholars have considered the possibility that the recipients being waited upon represented a mixed audience each attempting to remain exclusive. Both groups had been excluded from the Temple and its alms distribution, yet they were unable to share the community meals provided by the followers of Jesus.

The Hellenists complained that their widows were neglected in the distribution of food. The surviving spouse had been a member of the community by virtue of marriage. That the surviving spouse was being treated as if a non-member may suggest that the surviving spouse was not "Jewish" and further suggest that intermarriage was the issue lurking in the background that had resulted in the problem described in Acts.

Tyson explains:

> In Luke-Acts, widow means grief, poverty, vulnerability and piety. The exclusion of the widows from the common meal would, therefore, appear as an act of extreme cruelty and impiety, but also as a condition that underlined the urgent need for a solution. The reader should recognize immediately that here is an intolerable situation, one which can have only one solution: the widows must not be excluded.[49]

---

46. Acts 9:15 RSV.
47. Samaritans considered themselves to be "the sons of Israel."
48. Seland, *Hellenists, Hebrews, and Stephen*, 180.
49. Tyson, Acts 6:1–7 and Dietary Regulations, 158.

The Appointment of the Seven

"According to the Talmud, Pharisaism made little secret of its contempt for Hellenists and, unlike those from Syria or Babylonia (regions that are often considered extensions of the Holy Land in Talmudic discussions), they were frequently categorized by the native-born . . . populace of Jerusalem as second-class Israelites."[50]

Verse 6:1 is the most difficult verse in Acts. Consequently, the resolution of this enigma requires us to consider new ideas and revisit old ideas not properly developed.

Facts ignored by the traditional view of Acts 6

The following facts have been ignored in the analysis performed to ascertain the identity of the two groups in Acts 6:1.

1. Stephen is not identified by Luke as a Hellenist; Barnabas is the only person identified as a Hellenist;
2. the differences between the Hellenists and the Hebrews are not merely linguistic;
3. Luke considered both the Hebrews and Hellenists to be followers of Jesus;
4. the two groups receiving daily distributions have been denied access to the Temple;
5. the Hellenists of Acts 6 are not the same Greeks who disputed with Stephen and, in fact, there is no stated connection between them;
6. the call to "wait on tables" is about the continuation of a ministry of table fellowship with the outcasts and the oppressed begun by Jesus;
7. the Greeks disputing with Stephen accused him of having table fellowship with outcasts;
8. Acts 2:5 and 8:2 is an *inclusio*;
9. Acts 6:15 and 7:55 is also an *inclusio*;

---

50. Longenecker, *Commentary, Acts*, 125.

10. Stephen's speech contains a number of allusions to the Samaritan Pentateuch and theology; the SP contains the text of the Torah written in a special version of the early Hebrew script, preserved for centuries by the Samaritan community.

11. Acts 8:2 contains a rare word allusion to LXX Lev. 15:31 and LXX Micah 7:2;

12. Acts 8:2 also contains a rare word allusion to LXX Genesis 50:10 and 1 Maccabees 2:70; 4:39; 9:20 and 13:26; and

13. Luke has adopted a number of the literary patterns, themes, styles and techniques of the OT including hidden polemics involving the Samaritans and intermarriage.

During Roman times (fourth and fifth centuries CE), the Samaritan population is believed to have reached more than a million, but persecution, forced conversion, and forced migration by subsequent rulers and invaders decimated the population to the extent that they numbered 146 in the year 1917.

Samaritans were a sizable group of people speaking Hebrew who believed themselves to be the preservers of the original religion of ancient Israel. The name Samaritans literally from Hebrew means The Keepers (of original laws and traditions). Though it is difficult to speak of concrete numbers of the Samaritan population at the time of Jesus, it was comparable to those of the Jews and included large diaspora.

The Samaritans are direct descendants of the Northern Israelite tribes of Ephraim and Manasseh, who survived the destruction of the Northern Kingdom of Israel by the Assyrians in 722 B.C.E. Since Assyrian documents[51] of Sargon II record deporting a relatively small proportion of the Israelites (27,290), it is quite possible that a sizable population remained that could identify themselves as Israelites, the term that the Samaritans prefer for themselves.

Chronicles makes no mention of an Assyrian resettlement.[52] Yitzhak Magen argues that Chronicles is perhaps more accurate,

---

51. Sg II Nimrud Prism IV:25–41.
52. Magen, "Dating of the First Phase of the Samaritan Temple", 186.

The Appointment of the Seven

that the Assyrian settlement was unsuccessful, and that a notable Israelite population remained in Samaria, part of which, following the conquest of Judah, fled south, and settled there as refugees.[53]

There were Samaritans scattered all over the Roman world in the 1st century of our era. Only recently have historians begun to realize just how extensive the Samaritan population was in central Palestine, but also in Phoenicia, Egypt, Arabia, North Africa, Syria, Asia Minor, Greece, and even in Rome and throughout Italy. As for the population of the Samaritans, recent studies suggest that there were as many as half a million Samaritans in central Palestine in the 1st century and about three times that many in the other areas of the Roman Empire.[54] At least a third of the population of Caesarea in Palestine in the 1st century was Samaritan.[55] "Palestine before the destruction of the Temple had a population of about 2,500,000 including some 500,000 Samaritans, 'Greeks', and Nabateans. The capital, too, had grown considerably. Jerusalem's residents before the destruction of the Second Temple probably never exceeded 30,000 in number. Shortly before the end of the Second Commonwealth the city must have counted more than 120,000 inhabitants ascribed to it by Hecataeus[56] of Abdern three centuries earlier."[57]

Luke does not disclose that the Hebrews are Samaritans because

1. He assumed the designation was obvious;
2. He considered the Hebrews to be Jewish;
3. His sources did not disclose any missionary effort in Jerusalem among these two groups; and/or
4. Hidden polemic dictated that no disclosure be made.

---

53. Magen, "Dating of the First Phase of the Samaritan Temple", 187.
54. Crown, *Samaritans*, 201.
55. Crown, *Samaritans*, 206.
56. Hecateus cited in Ag. Ap. I, 22.197.
57. Baron, *Social and Religious History of the Jews*, 168.

It may be that Stephen is the product of a mixed marriage between a Hellenist and a Hebrew which would explain Luke's ambivalence concerning ethnic identity in part because the Samaritans are a patrilineal society while Judaism is a matrilineal society.

The apparent tranquility of the Jerusalem community of the followers of Jesus is deceptive and misleading.

Luke in 8:17 states: "For nothing is hidden that will not be disclosed, nor is anything secret that will not become known and come to light."

> Acts 6:2 And the Twelve summoned the body of the disciples and said, "It is not right that we should give up preaching the word of God to serve tables...."
>
> 6:2 τοὺς Ἑβραίους ὅτι παρεθεωροῦντο ἐν τῇ διακονίᾳ τῇ καθημερινῇ αἱ χῆραι αὐτῶν.

The Ἑλληνιστής and the Ἑβραῖος were both followers of Jesus because Luke tells us in verse 2 that "the twelve called together the body of disciples." The Ἑλληνιστής and the Ἑβραῖος together picked the seven men to wait on tables.

This verse reminds us that Jesus in Luke 22:27 asked the question "For which is the greater, one who sits at table, or one who serves?" In the Gospel of Luke, Jesus advocates what has been called servant leadership. One who wants to be leader must first be willing to serve. In Acts, we read that the Apostles "summoned the body of the disciples and said, 'It is not right that we should give up preaching the word of God to serve tables.'" In the story of appointment of the Seven, the Apostles have been placed in a bad light. Service is the driving motivation of Jesus and his followers in Luke.

This story confirms that there was a bit of tension within the movement when the Hellenists murmured against the Hebrews because the widows were being neglected. The tensions existed in part because the Samaritans were doing the neglecting. It is worth noting that Luke considers this dispute to be within the movement but does not consider the Samaritans to be Jewish.

The Appointment of the Seven

> Acts 6:3 Therefore, brethren, pick out from among you seven men of good repute, full of the Spirit and of wisdom, whom we may appoint to this duty.
>
> 6:3 ἐπισκέψασθε οὖν, ἀδελφοί ἄνδρας ἐξ ὑμῶν μαρτυρουμένους ἑπτὰ πλήρεις πνεύματος Ἁγίου καὶ σοφίας οὓς καταστήσομεν ἐπὶ τῆς χρείας ταύτης

As noted by Talbert, citing *Ant.* 4.214, Town Councils of seven men were common administrative entities in first century Judaism.[58]

Tannehill noted that "The stress on 'wisdom' is the most striking, as σοφίας is found only four times in Acts, and with all these occurrences in chapter 6 & 7 (6:3,10; 7:10,22)."[59] Wisdom was a characteristic of the Prophet Jesus who promised such wisdom to his disciples. It was also a characteristic of Jesus' prophetic predecessors, Joseph (7:10) and Moses (7:22).

The appointment of the Seven also recalls the appointment of the seventy helpers for Moses in Num. 11:11-13. That the Seven is a formal designation is probably shown by Acts 21:8.

The expression "full" (πλήρεις) of the "Holy Spirit" (πνεύματος Ἁγίου) and Lk 4:1 is related to prophetic inspiration in Acts 6:3, 10; 7:55. Those who are "full of the holy Spirt" are those who are fulfilling their Anointed tasks as proclaimers.

> Acts 6:4 But we will devote ourselves to prayer and to the ministry[60] of the word[61]."
>
> 6:4 ἡμεῖς δὲ τῇ προσευχῇ καὶ τῇ διακονίᾳ τοῦ λόγου προσκαρτερήσομεν

Luke uses the phrase "word of God" for the entire mission (4:32; 6:2, 7; 8:14; 11:1; 12:24; 19:20). Thus "ministry" probably means more than simply preaching. In Acts 1:14 it is said of the Apostles that "they continued steadfastly in prayer." They observed

---

58. Talbert, *Reading Acts*, 59.
59. Tannehill, *Narrative Unity*, Vol. 2, 83.
60. G1248 διακονία LXX none; M & M, 149.
61. The phrase "ministry of the word" appears once in RSV.

the Jewish times of prayer and devoted themselves to the ministry of teaching the word. Alongside proclamation of the message, prayer constituted a significant portion of the Apostles' activity. Schlatter indicates the appointment of the Seven was "carefully tailored to fit the needs of the Community."[62]

Unfortunately, there are no references to teaching at meals in Acts 6. However, we do have Act 2:42 which states: And they devoted themselves to the apostles' teaching and fellowship, to the breaking of bread and the prayer" which would suggest that the conflict occurred because there was no teaching and fellowship in the Hebrew Hellenist meal setting. This is supported by the recognition that διακονίᾳ is not "distribution" but "ministry." Within Acts, the RSV usually translates διακονίᾳ as ministry: 1:17, 25; 6:4, 20, 24; 21:19.

It is generally believed that "the mission among non-Jews begins with Philip outside Jerusalem."[63] This statement presumes that the people being served food in Jerusalem by the community are all Jewish. Perhaps the mission in Jerusalem did not evangelize the poor people who had been excluded from the Temple. Therefore, διακονίᾳ means "distribution" not "ministry."

> Acts 6:5 And what they said pleased the whole multitude, and they chose Stephen, a man full of faith and of the Holy Spirit, and Philip, and Proch'orus, and Nica'nor, and Ti'mon, and, Par'menas, and Nicola'us, a proselyte of Antioch.

> 6:5 Καὶ ἤρεσεν ὁ λόγος ἐνώπιον παντὸς τοῦ πλήθους; καὶ ἐξελέξαντο Στέφανον, ἄνδρα πλήρης πίστεως καὶ Πνεύματος Ἁγίου, καὶ Φίλιππον, καὶ Πρόχορον, καὶ Νικάνορα, καὶ Τίμωνα, καὶ Παρμενᾶν, καὶ Νικόλαον προσήλυτον Ἀντιοχέα,

Stephen and six other members of the community are elected to wait on tables. The criteria set forth in 6:3 is prophetic. The seven chosen are to be πλήρεις πνεύματος καὶ σοφίας. According

---

62. Schlatter, *Theology of the Apostles*, 401.
63. Stegemann, *Jesus Movement*, 219.

to Craig S. Keener, "the food distribution program is assigned to seven Hellenists."[64]

Acts "repeatedly certifies its heroes by means of notices that they are all filled with the Holy Spirit: Peter (4:8); Stephen (6:5, 7:55)."[65]

In Acts 6:5 faith enables the Spirit to move in new directions. In Acts 11:24 and 15:9, as noted by Topel that new direction is towards the Gentiles.[66] *Contra* Topel, in Acts 6:5 that direction is not towards the Gentiles. The eschatological reversal announced in Luke's prologue has a shocking twist. The exact phrase "full of faith" appears once. In Acts 11:24 Barnabas is described as "a good man, full of the Holy Spirit and of faith." In Hebrews 10:22 we read the phrase "in full assurance of faith."

One measure of the advance of the Greek language is the introduction of Greek names. Hengel noted that many Jewish people adopted Greek names.[67] Several studies have shown the appearance of Greek names among the later Hasmoneans and the priesthood. For instance, Jason, the High Priest, changed his name from Jesus.[68] The mere fact that Luke addressed his gospel to Theophilus is evidence of the influence of Hellenism. Sepulchral inscriptions probably best indicate the language of the common people.[69]

Therefore. it is significant that the vast majority of those published are in Greek.[70] Further evidence is shown by that "The fact that--to judge from other papyri--at least three-fourths of the Egyptian Jews had personal names of Greek, rather than Hebrew, origin is significant."[71]

"The solution for Luke is for the disadvantaged group to take over the task of justly distributing the provisions among the

---

64. Keener, *Acts, Commentary*, 1279.
65. Brawley, *Luke-Acts and the Jews*, 24.
66. Topel, *Children of a Compassionate God*, 244.
67. Hengel, *Judaism and Hellenism*, 69.
68. Jeremias, *Jerusalem*, 377.
69. Leon, *Jews of Rome*, 75.
70. Stambaugh, *NT in its Social Environment*, 87.
71. Baron, *Social and Religious History of the Jews*, 375.

congregation's members." Loring further states: "The office of economic leadership is distinguished from the primarily spiritual office of the 'Twelve.'"[72] However, "Munck rightly cautions against a too-facile assumption on the basis of Gr. names of all seven men chosen were Hellenists (which, of course allows him, together with C.S. Mann to view Stephen and Philip as Hebraic members of the Jewish Christian community)."[73]

The seven all had Greek names; Bruce[74] surmised that the seven were the leaders of the Hellenists. Bock states "Since the problem involves Hellenists, Hellenists are given the responsibility to solve it."[75]

> Acts 6:6 These they set before the apostles, and they prayed and laid their hands upon them.
>
> 6:6 οὓς ἔστησαν ἐνώπιον τῶν ἀποστόλων; καὶ προσευξάμενοι, ἐπέθηκαν αὐτοῖς τὰς χεῖρας.

As Gen. 48.14ff. indicates, "the laying on of hands was essentially enacted prayer, one achieved what was requested. The action did not just *accompany* the prayer, it was part of the prayer itself."[76]

In the context of Acts 6:3, 5, the laying on of hands by the Apostles signifies that these men have been endowed with the Holy Spirit and have been appointed as representation of the community with the expectation that God will bless them in their new role. The "laying on of hands" signifies to the community that these men are now designated agents of God. These seven men have been appointed as 'ministers' of the Word, to proclaim the Gospel, preach, and teach.

> Acts 6:7 And the word of God increased; and the number of the disciples multiplied greatly in Jerusalem, and a great many of the priests were obedient to the faith.

---

72. Löning, The Circle of Stephen, as to both quotes, 105–6.
73. Longenecker, *Acts* 128, note 5.
74. Bruce, *Acts* 183.
75. Bock, *Baker Commentary*, 261.
76. Banks, *Paul's Idea of Community*, 10.

The Appointment of the Seven

6:7 Καὶ ὁ λόγος τοῦ Θεοῦ ηὔξανεν, καὶ ἐπληθύνετο ὁ ἀριθμὸς τῶν μαθητῶν ἐν Ἰερουσαλὴμ σφόδρα; πολύς τε ὄχλος τῶν ἱερέων ὑπήκουον τε τῇ πίστει.

Luke intends to make a comparison between the growth of the Jesus movement and the situation in Israel in Exodus.

Bock states "The way the problem is eventually solved indicates it may well have surfaced not because of ethnic malice but because of lack of administrative organization caused by the new community's growth across diverse ethnic lines."[77]

Perhaps these priests are some of the poor rural priests serving in the temple mentioned by Josephus (Ant. 20.180–181). They were attracted to the soup kitchen and its ministry. This unlikely success story, told in summary form, may have caused a violent reaction resulting in the stoning of Stephen. In Luke-Acts the priesthood helps bolster the church's claim to be the heir of Israel's salvation history.

This verse is the first of six progress reports in Acts (6:7; 9:31; 12:54; 16:5; 19:20; and 28:31). Turner states that Acts is divided into six panels covering roughly five years each.[78]

Bruce believes that many priests joining "The adhesion of so many priests would strengthen the ties which bound a large proportion of the believers to the temple order; this would heighten the tension between them and those Hellenists who shared Stephen's negative assessment of the temple."[79] However, it should be noted the disciples were praying in the temple every day. Thus, Bruce's priests belong to Group 1.

Krodel's comment is interesting. "As believing priests, Luke seems to tell us, they shared Stephen's view of the temple."[80]

Are the Hebrews pro-temple and the Hellenists anti-temple? Bruce and Krodel fail to realize that both the Hellenists and the Hebrews are outcasts who have been excluded from the temple.

---

77. Bock, *Baker Commentary*, 258.
78. Turner, *Chronology*, 421–23.
79. Bruce, *Acts*, 185.
80. Krodel, *Acts*, 34.

Chapter 2

Stephen

> Acts 6:8 And Stephen, full of grace and power, did great wonders and signs among the people.
>
> 6:8 Στέφανος δὲ, πλήρης χάριτος καὶ δυνάμεως, ἐποίει τέρατα καὶ σημεῖα μεγάλα ἐν τῷ λαῷ.

The phrase, "wonders and signs," occurs 4 times in the RSV but only in Acts[1]. The more common phrase "signs and wonders" appears 30 times in the RSV including 4 times in Acts[2].

Only Stephen was described as "full of grace and power" who "did great wonders and signs among the people." God's power is evident in the miracles performed by his representatives and is a validation of their role. Acts 14:3; 14:8–11 and 15:12 makes it clear that these signs and wonders were performed by God acting through his designated agents.

Strelan has suggested that Stephen may be a priest. In support thereof, he states: "Stephen, like the priests of Israel, obviously knows the tradition and can recall and relate it; but not only does he retell it, he interprets it. He is not reprimanded by his superiors in the Sanhedrin (which included priests) for doing something he

---

1. Verses 2:22; 2:43; 6:18; 7:36
2. Verses 4:30; 5:12; 14:3; 15:12.

STEPHEN

had no authority to do. He was a legitimate controller and 'owner' of the tradition."[3]

> Acts 6:9 Then some of those who belonged to the synagogue of the Freedmen (as it was called), and of the Cyre'nians, and of the Alexandrians, and of those from Cili'cia and Asia, arose and disputed with Stephen.
>
> 6:9 ἀνέστησαν δέ τινες τῶν ἐκ τῆς συναγωγῆς τῆς λεγομένης Λιβερτίνων, καὶ Κυρηναίων καὶ Ἀλεξανδρέων καὶ τῶν ἀπὸ Κιλικίας καὶ Ἀσίας, συζητοῦντες τῷ Στεφάνῳ.

When Diaspora Jews moved back to Jerusalem, "each group had its own synagogue before they became Christians."[4] Jewish people of Hellenistic origin in Jerusalem built their own synagogues. Hemer indicates "it seems mostly likely that only one synagogue is meant, and possibly it is to be identified with that of Theodotus in the Opel inscription, certainly pre-70 (CIJ 4004)."[5]

The opponents of Stephen were members of diaspora synagogues in Jerusalem. A first century inscription, discovered by Raymond Weill in 1913–1914 in the lower City of David, confirmed the existence of a Greek-speaking synagogue in Jerusalem.[6] The plaque identifies Theodotos, son of Vettenus as a founder, priest and the head of the synagogue, ἀρχισυναγώγου, using the same Greek word that appears in Luke-Acts [Lk 8:49; 13:14; Acts 13:15; 18:8, 17]. The inscription credits the builder with the construction of a place for the reading and exposition of Torah, and included a hostel for pilgrims that was replete with guestrooms and "water installations." "Synagogue worship was unique" in that "it had no sacrificial component." Levine also notes that the inscription was significant because "it is written in Greek, as were about 35 percent of all Jerusalem inscriptions from the Second Temple period."[7]

---

3. Strelan, *Luke the Priest*, 127.
4. Kistemaker, *Commentary, Acts*, 220.
5. Hemer, *Acts in the Setting of Hellenistic History*, 176.
6. Charlesworth, *Jesus and Archaeology*, 50.
7. Stephen Levine, *Judaism & Hellenism*, 141 as to both quotes.

In Luke Acts the priesthood helps bolster the church's claim to be the heir of Israel's salvation history. (Lk 1:5 and Acts 6:9).

> Acts 6:10 But they could not withstand the wisdom and the Spirit with which he spoke.
>
> 6:10 καὶ οὐκ ἴσχυον ἀντιστῆναι τῇ σοφίᾳ καὶ τῷ Πνεύματι ᾧ ἐλάλει.

Stephen experienced the fulfillment of Jesus' promise in Luke 21:15 to give to his disciples "a mouth and wisdom, which none of your adversaries will be able to withstand or contradict."

> Acts 6:11 Then they secretly instigated[8] men, who said, "We have heard him speak blasphemous[9] words against Moses and God."
>
> 6:11 Τότε **ὑπέβαλον** ἄνδρας, λέγοντας ὅτι, Ἀκηκόαμεν αὐτοῦ λαλοῦντος ῥήματα **βλάσφημα** εἰς Μωϋσῆν καὶ τὸν Θεόν.

Acts 6:11–14, recall the story of Jez'ebel and Naboth which was about a religious conflict between the priests of YHWH and worshippers of the agricultural gods, Baal and Asherah. Luke thus alludes to idolatry which is addressed by Stephen in his speech. Jez'ebel had false witnesses instigates charges against Naboth so they could seize his vineyard.[10] The use of the Greek word for "blasphemous" is another allusion to idolatry. When two rare word allusions are made to idolatry in one verse, we can conclude that Luke intends this allusion.

> Acts 6:12 and they stirred up the people and the elders and the scribes, and they came upon him and seized him and brought him before the council,
>
> 6:12 συνεκίνησάν τε τὸν λαὸν καὶ τοὺς πρεσβυτέρους καὶ τοὺς γραμματεῖς, καὶ ἐπιστάντες, συνήρπασαν αὐτὸν καὶ ἤγαγον εἰς τὸ συνέδριον.

---

8. G5260 ὑποβάλλω LXX none; M & M, 656; Acts 6:11; to instigate secretly.
9. G989 βλάσφημος LXX Isa 66:3; M & M, 112; Acts 6:11.
10. Brodie, "The Accusing and Stoning of Naboth", 426.

This reminds us of the charge against Jesus that "he stirs up the people" (Ἀνασείει τὸν λαὸν Lk 23:5). The phrase "the elders and the scribes" recalls the arrest of Peter and John in Acts 4:5 and the speech Peter subsequently made to the Sanhedrin.

The scribes in Acts, as in the Gospel, are recognized and learned leaders of the community who are politically active in protecting the Jewish community.

In this verse Luke is describing a citizen's arrest.

Tarazi noted the parallel between Jeremiah's and Stephen's criticism of the Jerusalem Temple.[11] In both cases, a relatively few people stir up the crowds claiming that witnesses have heard blasphemous words.[12]

> Jer 26:11 Then the priests and the prophets said to the princes and all the people. 'This man deserves the sentence of death, because he prophesized against the city, as you have heard with your own ears.'

> Acts 6:13 and set up false[13] witnesses who said, "This man never ceases to speak words against this holy place and the law;

> 6:13 Ἔστησάν τε μάρτυρας ψευδεῖς, λέγοντας, Ὁ ἄνθρωπος οὗτος, οὐ παύεται λαλῶν ῥήματα κατὰ τοῦ τόπου τοῦ ἁγίου [τούτου] καὶ τοῦ νόμου;

> Psa 27:12 Give me not up to the will of my adversaries; for false witnesses have risen against me, and they breathe out violence.

The phrase "false witnesses" μάρτυρας ψευδεῖς alludes to Psalm 27:12 where the witnesses μάρτυρες are described by the word ἄδικοι which is descriptive of one who violates or has violated justice by deceitful testimony. Charry, discussing Ps 27:12, indicates "false, or at least exaggerated, accusations now apparently massed against him."[14]

---

11. Tarazi, *Luke and Acts*, 204.
12. Tarazi, *Luke and Acts*, 206.
13. G5571 ψευδής LXX numerous; M & M, 697; Acts 6:13.
14. Charry, *Psalms 1–50* (2015), 140.

> Acts 6:14 for we have heard him say that this Jesus of Nazareth will destroy this place, and will change the customs[15] which Moses delivered to us."
>
> 6:14 ἀκηκόαμεν γὰρ αὐτοῦ λέγοντος ὅτι Ἰησοῦς ὁ Ναζωραῖος οὗτος καταλύσει τὸν τόπον τοῦτον καὶ ἀλλάξει τὰ ἔθη ἃ παρέδωκεν ἡμῖν Μωϋσῆς.

"The Dead Sea Scrolls contains a passage openly hostile to the present temple but speaks of a future temple that will not be built with human hands. The tension between the present and future temple is further apparent in Jesus' saying that he will destroy this temple that is made with hands and build another, not made with hands."[16]

Stephen is accused of attacking the most fundamental pillars of Jewish identity and having associated with the condemned Jesus of Nazareth.[17]

Luke does not tell us what Stephen taught. Stephen does not mention any postexilic events. Luke, with his two rare word allusions in verse 6:11, made dual references to the pervasive idolatry. The Temple in Jerusalem was the primary reason for the hostility and divisions between Jerusalem and Samaria. No mission to Samaria could be successful unless followers of Jesus disassociated themselves from the cult on Mount Zion. Just like Jesus, Stephen substituted Moses and the prophets for Moses and the Temple. The successful mission in Samaria followed the death of Stephen.

> Acts 6:15 And gazing[18] at him, all who sat in the council saw that his face was like the face of an angel.
>
> 6:15 καὶ ἀτενίσαντες εἰς αὐτὸν ἅπαντες οἱ καθεζόμενοι ἐν τῷ συνεδρίῳ εἶδον τὸ πρόσωπον αὐτοῦ ὡσεὶ **πρόσωπον ἀγγέλου**

---

15. G1485 ἔθος LXX none; M & M 181.
16. Flusser, *Judaism of the Second Temple Period*, Vol. 2, 32–33.
17. Seland, *Hellenists, Hebrews, and Stephen*, 189.
18. G816 ἀτενίζω LXX none; M & M, 89; Lk 4:20; 22:56; Acts 6:15; 7:55.

Stephen

The members of the Sanhedrin see a change in the appearance of Stephen's face. Luke is clearly comparing Stephen to Moses whose "face shone because he had been talking with God"[19] and to Jesus at the Transfiguration.[20] It emphasizes the presence of God. The description of Stephen's face looking like "the face of an angel" is unique in the Greek scriptures. The transfiguration signifies that Stephen is an authoritative agent of God.

"Particularly interesting, in view of the issue for which Stephen is on trial, is the Targum to the Song of Songs (1:5) where Israel's obedience to the Torah at Sinai means that 'the splendour of the glory of their face was as great as that of the angels.'"[21] Fletcher-Louis also stated "there is connection with Acts 7:53 in that the giving of the law by the angelomorphic Stephen.

The two references create an *inclusio* round the lengthy speech in Acts 7:1–53. Stephen speaks against the Torah (6:11, 13); he answered with the accusation that his accusers do not themselves keep the torah."[22]

In a footnote Flecher-Louis cited Scharlemann who stated:

> the expression is probably best understood in light of a statement such as that of the Targum on Canticles, to the effect that, when the people of Israel had finished making the golden calf, their faces turned black like those of the sons of Cush, but that when they repented and received forgiveness, a splendor covered their countenances like that of the angels.[23]

Exodus 34:35 καὶ εἶδον οἱ υἱοὶ Ισραηλ τὸ πρόσωπον Μωυσῆ ὅτι δεδόξασται καὶ περιέθηκεν Μωυσῆς κάλυμμα ἐπὶ τὸ **πρόσωπον** ἑαυτοῦ ἕως ἂν εἰσέλθῃ συλλαλεῖν αὐτῷ

Exodus 34:35 the people of Israel saw the face of Moses, that the skin of Moses' face shone; and Moses would put

---

19. Exo 34:29.
20. Lk 9:29.
21. Fletcher-Louis, *Luke-Acts: Angels*, 97.
22. Fletcher-Louis, *Luke-Acts: Angels*, 98.
23. Scharlemann, *Stephen*, 14.

the veil upon his face again, until he went in to speak with him.

Luke 9:29 καὶ ἐγένετο ἐν τῷ προσεύχεσθαι αὐτὸν τὸ εἶδος τοῦ **προσώπου** αὐτοῦ ἕτερον καὶ ὁ ἱματισμὸς αὐτοῦ λευκὸς ἐξαστράπτων

Luke 9:29 And as he was praying, the appearance of his countenance was altered, and his raiment became dazzling white.

In Acts 6:15, Exodus 34;34 and Luke 9:29 προσώπου is translated as face.

Chapter 3

Accusation

Acts 7:1 And the high priest said, "Is this so?"

7:1 Εἶπεν δὲ ὁ ἀρχιερεύς, Εἰ ταῦτα οὕτως ἔχει ;

Most of the commentators do not discuss the identity of the unnamed high priest who addressed Stephen: "Is this so?" The reason Luke does not explicitly name the high priest concerns the irenical purpose of his message. For the same reason, Luke does not explicitly identify Caiaphas as the name of the High Priest before Jesus appeared.

In my view, the stoning of Stephen occurs during the high priesthood of Jonathan. This proposal causes problems for most if not all Pauline chronology schemes except possibly Robin Lane Fox. The high priesthood of Jonathan can be precisely dated using the information from Josephus. For Josephus, there are three great holidays: the pilgrimage festivals of Passover, Shavuot, also known as Pentecost and *Sukkot*[1], when all Jews were enjoined to travel to Jerusalem to perform the necessary sacrifices and rites at the Temple. Since Josephus mentions that Jonathan is appointed High Priest at the time of Passover, his removal either occurred at the time of Shavuot, seven weeks later or *Sukkot*, five months

---

1. *Sukkot*, usually translated as "Tabernacles," or the festival of "Booths."

later. The Hebrew feast of Shavuos, the Festival of Weeks, appears five times in the works of Josephus, who calls it by its Greek name Pentecost. Josephus identifies the removal event as follows: Vitellius "went up to Jerusalem to offer sacrifice to God, an ancient festival of the Jews then approaching."[2] In agreement with Jeremias, *Sukkot* is the more likely ancient festival being identified by Josephus. Stephen used Nehemiah 9 as the model and source for his sermon perhaps because the events described therein immediately followed the Festival of Sukkot. According to Ezra (3:4) and Nehemiah (8:14–15) the returnees celebrated the holiday of Sukkot according to the law as it "was written."

There is additional circumstantial evidence supporting the identification of Jonathan and the time period as the time period of the stoning of Stephen. Another son of Annas served for a brief time during the sixties as high priest and during his high priesthood the stoning of James occurred. The following similarities should be noted:

> Jonathan + Ananus
> son of Annas + son of Annas
> 5 months, 37 C.E. + 3 months, 62 C.E.
> Vitellius in Antioch + Albinius out of town
> stoning of Stephen + stoning of James
> removal + removal

These two events occurred during a period of time when the Sanhedrin was unable to impose a death sentence without Roman approval. This should serve as a clue as to what happened in 37 C.E. In the case of James, the reigning high priest was removed as soon as Albinius arrived in Jerusalem. Festus died in office in 62 C.E. The Emperor Nero sends Albinius to replace Festus. At the same time, King Agrippa II who had been granted control over the high priesthood bestows it on Ananus. Josephus describes Ananus as rash and impertinent. Josephus further states that he "followed the school of the Sadducees, who, when it comes to judgments, are

---

2. Ant. 18.122.

ACCUSATION

savage beyond all other Jews as I have explained."[3] Josephus then relates the stoning of James, brother of Jesus. Before Albinius can act, King Agrippa removes Ananus as High Priest. The account in Josephus can be interpreted to mean that the High Priest was responsible for maintaining order and perhaps seek approval of the Romans prior to the imposition of the death sentence.

With respect to Stephen, we know that Jonathan served as High Priest for about 5 months before he was removed and replaced by his brother. Josephus does not tell us the reason for this unusual change of high priest after a brief period of service in that Jonathan did not die in office and we are left to speculate as to the reason for his removal. We do know that according to Acts, Stephen was stoned, and the High Priest was involved. This High Priest was Jonathan. Just prior to the removal of the High Priest, there was vacuum in power as the top Roman official assigned to Judea was out of town. Pilate was on his way to Rome, probably in chains and Vitellius was in Antioch.

In both situations, perhaps the reigning High Priest took advantage of the situation. Jonathan was removed as High Priest because the stoning of Stephen took place on his watch and the Roman official took offense because he considered it to be a usurpation of his power. The stoning either was considered a 'loss of control of the crowds' or 'failure to seek Roman approval of the death sentence.' Josephus mentions another instance where the High Priest was removed because an event occurred for which he was held responsible: the removal of the eagle at the Temple in the last days of Herod the Great when Matthias was the High Priest.[4]

In both instances, it would fair to infer that the stoning occurred because both Stephen and James had been publicly blaming the Temple establishment for the death of Jesus. As noted, this identification is problematical, not for any logical reason but solely because it interferes with the pet theories about Pauline chronology. All Pauline chronologies, except for Robin Lane Fox, start with Paul's conversion in 33/34 C.E.

3. Ant. 20.197.
4. VanderKam, From Joshua to Caiaphas, 412.

Josephus does not tell us the reason why Jonathan only served five months. The reason is easy to understand. For Josephus, Jonathan is one of the good guys. There is simply no event prior to the high priesthood of Jonathan that can serve as the setting for the stoning of Stephen.

In Acts 4:5–6, we read:

> On the morrow their rulers and elders and scribes were gathered together in Jerusalem, with Annas the high priest and Caiaphas and John and Alexander, and all who were of the high priestly family.

Luke does not mean to say that Annas was the reigning High Priest; rather Annas is named as the High Priest by Luke because

1. he is considered by Jewish society to still be the High Priest, as High Priest for life;
2. because he is the power behind the throne;
3. as a mark of respect due the former High Priest; and
4. as part of the irenical presentation that Luke is making to Theophilus, the High Priest, son of Annas.

This is not to say that Annas was the reigning High Priest when Jesus appeared before him or when Stephen was stoned. This is consistent with Luke's usage in Lk. 3:2 and consistent with Josephus' usage in identifying a former High Priest as High Priest.

This John in Acts 4:5–6 should be correctly identified as Jonathan. In fact, the Western text[5] has the name correctly as Jonathan, which would be consistent with Josephus[6] who identifies Jonathan as the high priest who follows Caiaphas. One commentator notes that "This sort of inconsequential detail, the mentioning of names that do not really play a role in the narrative, is characteristic of Luke and suggest his use of sources."[7] On the contrary, "this sort of inconsequential detail" is a hint of the

---

5. Metzger, Textual Commentary on the Greek New Testament, 317.
6. Ant.18.4.3.
7. Witherington, Acts, 191.

ACCUSATION

greater involvement of Jonathan in a subsequent event consistent with Luke's step-progression method. Krodel claims "Luke never says everything at once, but expands and unfolds earlier themes as he moves step by step from one episode to another."[8] Based on the above, the date of Paul's conversion cannot be earlier than 37 C.E.

"The most remarkable element in Acts 7:2–8, in contrast with similar summaries, is the prominent place given to a full quotation of Genesis 15:13–14, with some important variations."[9]

---

8. Krodel, Acts, 281.
9. Dahl, Memory, 72.

Chapter 4

Abraham

Acts 7:2 And Stephen said: "Brethren and fathers, hear me. The God of glory appeared to our father Abraham, when he was in Mesopota'mia, before he lived in Haran,

7:2 ὁ δὲ ἔφη Ἄνδρες ἀδελφοὶ καὶ πατέρες ἀκούσατε Ὁ θεὸς τῆς δόξης ὤφθη τῷ πατρὶ ἡμῶν Ἀβραὰμ ὄντι ἐν τῇ Μεσοποταμίᾳ πρὶν ἢ κατοικῆσαι αὐτὸν ἐν Χαρράν

In LXX Gen 12:7 we found the expression "the LORD appeared to Abraham."

The word doxa (glory), is closely connected with the theme of God's presence or dwelling among his people.

"The speech is the longest and perhaps most perplexing address in Acts."[1]

The salvation history narrative which Stephen addressed to the Sanhedrin in the temple precinct in Hebrew unites Moses, Jesus and the speaker with the prophetic theme of miracle and rejection that Dillon identified.[2]

Stephen's response takes the form of a selective retelling of Israel's history. "For much of the speech there is a sense that

---

1. Soards, The Speeches in Acts, 58.
2. Dillon, From Eye-Witness to Ministers of the Word, 123–124.

ABRAHAM

Stephen and his audience share a common heritage, and we have a number of expressions such as 'our race' (7:19) and 'our fathers' (7:11–12, 15, 19, 38–39, 44–45)."[3] The speech contains four quotations of and numerous allusions to scripture, most of them from the Samaritan Pentateuch, with detailed references to Abraham, Moses and Joseph. But the speech, which is more than a simple recital of Hebrew history, "uses a technique familiar in the OT and post-OT Jewish writings, by putting a theological statement in the form of a speech or song recounting the history of Israel from ancient times."[4] Unlike other retellings, this speech ends with a condemnation of the people and the temple establishment. "In Acts alone, the author has explicitly quoted twenty passages from the Septuagint."[5] In Chapter 7, Stephen cites Gen. 15:13–14 (Acts 7:6–7); Exod 3:12 (Acts 7:7); Isa 66:1–2 (Acts 7:49–50); and Amos 5:25–27 (Acts 7:42–43).[6] All of the quotations with the exception of Acts 8:22 occur in speeches.

The three great pillars of second temple Judaism were the land, the law and the Temple. Stephen begins his defense with a retelling of the history of The Promised Land, the giving of the Law at Sinai and the building of the Temple in Jerusalem. This retelling was unique in several respects prompting the following observations:

1. the speech is framed with glory and

2. begins and continues with references to God appearing to and speaking with His chosen servants in sacred space outside the Promised Land;

3. Stephen presented the message of the rejected prophets and of the people "who stopped their ears" to that message;

4. Stephen made a number of explicit and implicit allusions to matters of Samaritan interests, including but not limited to,

---

3. Tyson, Images of Judaism in Luke-Acts, 113.
4. Maddox, The Purpose of Luke-Acts, 52.
5. Pao, Acts and the Isaianic New Exodus, 4.
6. Acts and the Isaianic New Exodus, 4.

mentioning Haran (7:2, 4), Joseph (7:9–16), Shechem (7:7, 16), Moses, the sons of Israel (7:23), and "this place";

5. Stephen demonstrated that the inclination of the people has always been to worship and love "the work of their own hands," (vs. 41);
6. the most significant aspect about the tabernacle is the absence of any tie to a specific geographical location;
7. not only was the temple in the wrong place but the temple in Jerusalem was made with human hands;
8. the inclusion of foreigners used a Samaritan argument about sacred space and place; and
9. Stephen, as a chosen servant, presented a brilliant defense of the son of man that cost the Samaritan preacher his life and provided the inspiration and source for the theology that replaced the land, law and Temple.

The initial address in v.2, "men, brothers and fathers, listen" is employed by Stephen to establish rapport with his audience. Witherington notes this is "the proper rhetorical approach."[7] Stephen then says, "the God of glory appeared to our father Abraham." The speech includes ἀκούσατε, listen, six times and ends by the narrator saying, "when they heard these things, they became enraged and ground their teeth at him," (7:54).

The phrase "the God of glory" is unique in the NT and found only in LXX Psalm 28:3. Stephen not only borrowed the phrase, but also the format, which he observed in the psalm's sevenfold repetition of "the voice of God." With this six-fold usage, ἀκούσατε, listen, Stephen reminds his audience that God is the supreme ruler of the world and "that God controls not only nature but also history."[8] In agreement with Gerhard Krodel, "the God of glory is the theme of this speech."[9] The speech "disclosed that

---

7. Witherington, 264.
8. Charry, 148.
9. Krodel, Acts, 140.

salvation history is also a history of failure to respond to 'the God of glory.'"[10]

Stephen may have alluded to Ezekiel 44. Initially, although "the God of glory" is an explicit allusion to Ps 28:3 LXX, 29:3 MT, it is also likely that Stephen and his audience was associating the glory of God — the Shekinah — with the moveable tabernacle in the wilderness (Exodus 25:8; 40:34-38), and later the temple (Ezekiel 43:2, 4). In same vein, the "living oracle" (Acts 7:38) may allude to the vision of the prophet in Ezekiel 44 and "uncircumcised of heart" may allude to "uncircumcised in heart" in Ezekiel 44:9.

In addition, Michael Fishbane described Ezekiel 44:9-16 as "an exegetical oracle."[11] As MacDonald stated: "There is almost no part of Ezekiel 44 that does not draw upon another text from elsewhere in the Hebrew Bible: Gen 17; Lev 10, 21-22; Numbers 15, 18; Deut 18; Isaiah 56: Ezekiel 14."[12] This unusual text, containing a graphically vivid divine oracle, may have been the source of the idea of Stephen to include numerous biblical allusions in his speech.

An angelic figure leads Ezekiel on a tour of the future temple wherein the prophet witnesses the return of YHWH's glory to the sanctuary. This angelic tour is the basis of the idea that "the God of glory" inhabits the Temple rebuilt by Nehemiah. Ezekiel 44 contains the word of judgment (vv. 10, 12, 15) describing Israel's preference for idol worship just as Psalm 28 LXX was critical of Canaanite Baal worship.

It is likely that "the God of glory" allusion to Psalm 29 was offensive. This psalm "was probably written as a polemical rejoinder to Canaanite Baal worship (and remind Israel) that the LORD God of Israel is the one true God."[13] "While the immediate target population is the Canaanites, it also targets Israel, which is constantly tempted by its neighbors' religious practices."[14] The Sanhedrin

10. Krodel, 131.
11. Fishbane, Biblical Interpretation in Ancient Israel, 138.
12. MacDonald, Priestly Rule, 149.
13. Charry, 148.
14. Charry, 151.

recognized that Stephen is using the phrase "the God of glory" to tell them his response is about their idolatrous religious practices which are like the Canaanites.

> Act 7:3 and said to him, 'Depart from your land and from your kindred[15] and go into the land which I will show you.'
>
> Acts 7:3 καὶ εἶπεν πρὸς αὐτόν·**Ἔξελθε ἐκ τῆς γῆς σου καὶ ἐκ τῆς συγγενείας σου** καὶ δεῦρο **εἰς γῆν ἣν ἄν σοι δείξω**
>
> Gen 12:1 Now the LORD said to Abram, "Go from your country and your kindred and your father's house to the land that I will show you.
>
> Gen 12:1 καὶ εἶπεν κύριος τῷ Αβραμ **ἔξελθε ἐκ τῆς γῆς σου καὶ ἐκ τῆς συγγενείας σου** καὶ ἐκ τοῦ οἴκου τοῦ πατρός σου **εἰς τὴν γῆν ἣν ἄν σοι δείξω**

The bold type shows what Greek words are in both passages suggesting that Gen 12:1 was used as a source.

Abraham has been given a directive from God reminding the Sanhedrin of similar directives in Gen 12:1, Ex 33:1, 1 Sam 22:5 and 2 Kings 8:1.

In Acts 7:2–3 we read about God's initiative which is also stressed in Gen. 15:7; Neh. 9:7; Heb. 11:8 and Josephus' *Ant.* I.154.

> Acts 7:4 Then he departed from the land of the Chalde'ans, and lived in Haran. And after his father died, God removed[16] him (μετῴκισεν) from there into this land in which you are now living;
>
> 7:4 τότε ἐξελθὼν ἐκ γῆς Χαλδαίων κατῴκησεν ἐν Χαρράν. κἀκεῖθεν μετὰ ἀποθανεῖν τὸν πατέρα αὐτοῦ μετῴκισεν αὐτὸν εἰς τὴν γῆν ταύτην εἰς ἣν ὑμεῖς νῦν κατοικεῖτε.

Verse 4 contains a second mention of Haran (7:2 and 4), the place from which the Samaritans returned from exile.[17] In this verse, Stephen states that Abraham went to Canaan after the death

---

15. G4772 συγγένεια; numerous including 2 Macc. 8:1; Acts 7:3,14.
16. G3351 μετοικίζω remove; Acts 7:4,43.
17. See MacDonald, *The Theology of the Samaritans*, 20.

ABRAHAM

of Terah agreeing with the SP's statement that Terah died at the age of 145 years. Stern states that Stephen was using the SP.[18] In contrast, the MT and LXX both state Terah died at the age of 205 (Gen 11:32) sixty years after Abraham left. Stephen resolves a problem, created by Genesis (11:26,32; 12:4), with Abraham leaving after his father's death. In following the SP, Stephen avoids the appearance that Abraham had abandoned his father.

> Acts 7:5 yet he gave him no **inheritance** in it, **not even a foot's length**, but promised to give it to him in **possession**[19] and to his posterity after him, though he had no child.

> 7:5 καὶ οὐκ ἔδωκεν αὐτῷ **κληρονομίαν** ἐν αὐτῇ **οὐδὲ βῆμα ποδός** καὶ ἐπηγγείλατο αὐτῷ δοῦναι εἰς **κατάσχεσιν** αὐτὴν καὶ τῷ σπέρματι αὐτοῦ μετ' αὐτόν οὐκ ὄντος αὐτῷ τέκνου

The Greek phrase "οὐδὲ βῆμα ποδός" (not even a foot's length) appears in the LXX only in

> Deut 2:5 LXX do not contend with them; for I will not give you any of their land, no, not so much as for the sole of the foot to tread on, because I have given Mount Se'ir to Esau as a possession.

> 2:5 μὴ συνάψητε πρὸς αὐτοὺς πόλεμον οὐ γὰρ μὴ δῶ ὑμῖν ἀπὸ τῆς γῆς αὐτῶν **οὐδὲ βῆμα ποδός** ὅτι ἐν κλήρῳ δέδωκα τοῖς υἱοῖς Ησαυ τὸ ὄρος τὸ Σηιρ

> 2:5 SP Do not provoke them, for I will not give you any of their land as an inheritance, not even a treading of the foot sole. Because I have given Mount Sha'er to Ishaab as a possession.

The language of "inheritance" and "promise" is only found together in 2 Maccabees 2:17–18 and Acts 7:5.[20]

---

18. Jewish NT Commentary, 244. Tsedaka, Samaritan Torah, 26.
19. G2697 κατάσχεσις LXX numerous; Acts 7:5,45.
20. Johnson, Acts, 115

Act 7:6 And God spoke to this effect, that his **posterity** would be **aliens** in a **land** belonging to others, who would **enslave** them and **ill-treat** them for **four hundred years**.

7:6 ἐλάλησεν δὲ οὕτως ὁ θεὸς ὅτι ἔσται τὸ **σπέρμα** αὐτοῦ **πάροικον** ἐν γῇ ἀλλοτρίᾳ καὶ **δουλώσουσιν** αὐτὸ καὶ **κακώσουσιν ἔτη τετρακόσια**

Gen 15:13 Then the LORD said to Abram, "Know of a surety that your **descendants** will be **sojourners** in a **land** that is not theirs, **and will be slaves** there, and they will be **oppressed** for **four hundred years**;

15:13 καὶ ἐρρέθη πρὸς Αβραμ γινώσκων γνώσῃ ὅτι **πάροικον** ἔσται τὸ **σπέρμα** σου ἐν γῇ οὐκ

ἰδίᾳ **καὶ δουλώσουσιν** αὐτοὺς **καὶ κακώσουσιν** αὐτοὺς καὶ ταπεινώσουσιν αὐτοὺς **τετρακόσια ἔτη**.

Soards noted that J. Dupont suggests that vv. 6–7 set the structure of the major portion of the speech. Verse 6 anticipates vv. 9–22; v. 7a relates to vv. 23–44; and v. 7b anticipates vv. 44–50.[21]

Bock indicates "The figure in Acts is simply a rounded number, ..."[22] Lim indicates "The dating of the reception of the Torah at Sinai seems to follow the Septuagint of Ex 12:40 (tallying with 400 years of Egypt to Egypt of Genesis 15:13; so also Acts 7:6)."[23] Both the MT and SP have 430 years.

Acts 7:7 'But I will judge the nation which they serve,' said God, 'and after that they shall come out and **worship me in this place**.'

Acts 7:7 Καὶ τὸ ἔθνος ᾧ ἐὰν δουλεύσουσιν, κρινῶ ἐγώ, ὁ Θεὸς εἶπεν, Καὶ μετὰ ταῦτα ἐξελεύσονται λατρεύσουσίν μοι ἐν τῷ τόπῳ τούτῳ.

John Kilgallen[24] has probably written the most thorough and authoritative presentation of the Stephen Speech to date. Kilgallen

21. Soards, 62, Footnote 145.
22. Bock, *Baker Commentary*, 284.
23. Lim, Holy Scriptures in the Qumran Commentaries, 51, fn.9.
24. Kilgallen, Stephen Speech, 38.

made it very clear that Abram Spiro and Martin Scharlemann "have written so succinctly"[25] on the Samaritan relationship to the speech that he will not discuss further this Samaritan issue. Neither Kilgallen, Spiro nor Scharlemann discussed the true significance of verse 7 and how verse 7 supports a more focused interpretation of Samaritan influence of this speech. Consequently, we will be addressing the significance of verse 7 of the speech and explaining what Stephen meant when he said: 'and after that they shall come out and worship me in this place.'

Acts 7:7 conflates two passages, Genesis 15:14 and Exodus 3:12[26]. Luke changes the end of the citation of Gen 15:14 by changing 'with great possessions' to 'and worship me in this place.'"[27] Siker asserts that "The focus on *true* worship rather than the place of worship becomes clearer when attention is drawn to the parallels between Acts 7:6–7 and the Benedictus in Luke 1:68–75. In Luke 1:72–75 Zechariah praises God,

> to perform the mercy promised to our fathers, and to remember his holy covenant, the oath which he swore to our father Abraham, to grant us that we, being delivered from the hand of our enemies, might serve him without fear, in holiness and righteousness before him all the days of our life.

In the words of the Benedictus, we are delivered from our enemies to serve and worship the LORD."[28]

The phrase "'worship Me in this place (λατρεύσουσίν μοι ἐν τῷ τόπῳ τούτῳ)' combines God's appearance to Abraham (cf. Gen 15:14) with His appearance to Moses (cf. Ex. 3:12). Rather than saying that the people would come out 'with many possessions,' Stephen associates the Exodus with the giving of the Torah and God's proclamation to Moses that the people would "worship God at this mountain. . . ." The further change from "mountain" to

---

25. Kilgallen, Stephen Speech, 4.
26. Siker, Disinheriting the Jews, 122.
27. Siker, 122.
28. Siker, 123.

"place" focuses the attention on the place which the LORD God has chosen to place his name. In Judah and Judeans in the 4th century BCE, Yitzhak Magen states, "The inscriptions discovered on Mt. Gerizim are the most striking indication of the existence of the temple."[29] One inscription contains the formula "before God in this place."[30]

A considerable Israelite population remained in Samaria, and the Judean kings Hezekiah and Josiah took steps to draw them closer. Scripture has at least 170 references to the land that God gave to the offspring of Abraham, Isaac and Jacob. The earliest promise is found at Genesis 12:6–8. Consequently, the most logical question is what is the immediate antecedent of "this place" where Abram was when God "promised to give it to him in possession . . . ." "'In this place,' at the end of v 7b, must necessarily refer to the place where Abraham receives the declaration by God; that place is in Israel."[31] The Exodus text is reworked to apply it to the place where Abraham received the declaration instead of to Sinai.

When Abram leaves Haran for Canaan, he first arrives in the "Promised Land" at the plain of Moreh in Shechem (Gen 12:6–8). The bones are buried in Shechem. (Josh 24:32; cf. Exodus 13:19). Through covenant renewal ceremonies such as Joshua 24, the Bible connects God's covenant with Israel to Shechem long before Jerusalem becomes the city of David.

This place is identified in SP and MT Gen 12:6 as "Shechem, to the plain of Moreh." This is the place where the LORD appeared to Abram and said, "To your descendants I will give this land. So, he built there an altar to the LORD." The SP text states in Deuteronomy 27:4 that the altar was to be built on Mount Gerizim, shortly after the sons of Israel entered the holy land. Incidentally, this is the spot where Abram built an altar to the LORD. This is the point that Stephen is making when he says, "this place." This is the place being identified by Stephen in Acts 7:7 "'and after that they shall come out and **worship me in this place.**'" Shechem had

29. Magen, 166.
30. Magen, 167; "indicative of a temple".
31. Kilgallen, Stephen Speech, 38.

already been chosen at the time of the Patriarchs (Gen 12:6; Gen 33:18–20). Thus, while MT reads "the place which the LORD your God will choose" (Deut 12:5 and other verses in Deuteronomy), referring to Jerusalem, SP has "the place which the LORD your God has chosen" referring to Mount Gerizim.

Recently it has become increasing clear, with the writings of Schorch, Charlesworth, Ulrich, Tsedaka and Magen, that the SP Deut 27 is earlier than the MT and that Jerusalem scribes changed the MT reading of Deut 27:4 from Mount Gerizim to Mount Ebal. In 2011, Stefan Schorch, in a thorough study of Deuteronomy 27, "The Samaritan Version of Deuteronomy and the Origin of Deuteronomy", concluded that the Samaritan's version was the original and that Mount Gerizim is the place "He has chosen."[32] Benyamin Tsedaka, in his introduction to the first English translation of *The Israelite Samaritan Version of the Torah*, stated: "This new discovery from Qumran (Charlesworth), and the fact that the same reading for Deut 27:4–6 occurs also in *Vetus Latina* (as noted by Schorch and Ulrich) as well as the Samariticon, the Greek translation of the Samaritan Pentateuch, leads the translator to suggest that 'in Mount Gerizim' should no longer be considered a 'Samaritan correction' but should be regarded as an original Israelite text, dating many hundreds of years before the rise of the Jewish-Samaritan polemics of the Second Temple period."[33]

> Acts 7:8 And he gave him the **covenant of circumcision**. And so, Abraham became the father of Issac, circumcised him on the eighth day; and Isaac became the father of Jacob, and Jacob of the twelve patriarchs.
>
> Acts 7:8 καὶ ἔδωκεν αὐτῷ **διαθήκην περιτομῆς** καὶ οὕτως ἐγέννησεν τὸν Ἰσαὰκ καὶ περιέτεμεν αὐτὸν τῇ ἡμέρᾳ τῇ ὀγδόῃ καὶ ὁ Ἰσαὰκ τὸν Ἰακώβ καὶ ὁ Ἰακώβ τοὺς δώδεκα πατριάρχας.
>
> "And the uncircumcised male, who is not circumcised in the flesh of his foreskin on the eighth day, that soul

---

32. Schorch, "The Samaritan Version of Deuteronomy", 23–37.
33. Tsedaka, xxv.

> shall be cut off from his people, for he has broken my covenant." Gen 17:14 SP.

The Septuagint and Jub. 15:14 both includes the phrase "on the eighth day." The Masoretic test omits the phrase "on the eight day."

> Gen 17:13 both he that is born in your house and he that is bought with your money, shall be circumcised. So shall my covenant be in your flesh an everlasting covenant.

> 17:13 **περιτομῇ** περιτμηθήσεται ὁ οἰκογενὴς τῆς οἰκίας σου καὶ ὁ ἀργυρώνητος καὶ ἔσται ἡ **διαθήκη** μου ἐπὶ τῆς σαρκὸς ὑμῶν εἰς διαθήκην αἰώνιον

In Genesis 17:13, circumcision became the sign of the covenant. The expression **διαθήκην περιτομῆς** is unique to Stephen but the two Greek words do appear in Gen 17:13 but not together. These two words appear in the same Greek sentence only in Genesis 17:13 and Acts 7:8.

The *Hilluk*, the Samaritan Code of Law, provides:

> They, on the morning of this day, from the rising of the sun begin to circumcise the boy's foreskin. And he who is not circumcised on the eight day will be lost, and is not called by the name of Hebrew, nor is he clean.[34]

Only on the eighth is he to be circumcised, and it is not to be postponed. The Jewish community may delay up to 30 days.

The mention of circumcision served two purposes: 1) the covenant was being practiced before any land was owned by Abraham; and 2) Stephen upholds the covenant of circumcision and recognizes its validity outside the land. Many Greek speaking Jews denied the validity of circumcision. Thus, Stephen challenged the Hellenists even while undermining the tripod.

John the Baptist was circumcised on the eighth day[35] as was Jesus.[36] Circumcision was regarded as an essential part of Jewish practice.

---

34. Bowman, Samaritan Documents, 306.
35. Lk. 1:59.
36. Lk. 2:21.

CHAPTER 5

Joseph

Act 7:9 "And the patriarchs, jealous of Joseph, sold him into Egypt; but God was with him,

Acts 7:9 Καὶ οἱ πατριάρχαι, ζηλώσαντες τὸν Ἰωσὴφ, ο ἀπέδοντο εἰς Αἴγυπτον. καὶ ἦν ὁ Θεὸς μετ' αὐτοῦ,

THE expression "God was with him" appears in Gen 21:20; in 2 Ch 1:1 in reference to Solomon; and in 2 Ch 15:9 in reference to Asa.

In Gen 39:2–3 it is said twice of Joseph that "LORD was with him" and also in verses 21 and 23. This phrase is more commonly used than "God was with him." It appears 18 times in the RSV: Joseph (as mentioned above); Joshua (Jos 6:27); Judah (Judges 1:19); the judges (Judges 2:18); Samuel (1 Sam 3:19); Saul (1 Sa 18:12); David (1 Sa 18:12, 14, 28; 2 Sa 5:10); Hezeki'ah (2 Ki 18:7: Phin'ehas (1Ch 9:20); Jehosh'asphat (2 Ch 17:3); and Jesus (Lk 1:66; 5:17; Acts 10:38). When this phrase is said of a person more than once, as with David, Stephen and Jesus, it implies some divine favor has been accorded to a righteous person.

> Acts 7:10 and rescued him out of all his afflictions, and gave him favor and wisdom before Pharaoh, king of Egypt, who made him governor over Egypt and over all

his household." "and gave him favor" **"καὶ ἔδωκεν αὐτῷ χάριν"**

7:10 καὶ ἐξείλετο αὐτὸν ἐκ πασῶν τῶν θλίψεων αὐτοῦ **καὶ ἔδωκεν αὐτῷ χάριν** καὶ σοφίαν ἐναντίον Φαραὼ βασιλέως Αἰγύπτου καὶ κατέστησεν αὐτὸν ἡγούμενον ἐπ' Αἴγυπτον καὶ ὅλον τὸν οἶκον αὐτοῦ

Gen 39:21 But the LORD was with Joseph and showed him steadfast love, and gave him favor in the sight of the keeper of the prison.

Gen 39:21 καὶ ἦν κύριος μετὰ Ιωσηφ καὶ κατέχεεν αὐτοῦ ἔλεος **καὶ ἔδωκεν αὐτῷ χάριν** ἐναντίον τοῦ ἀρχιδεσμοφύλακος

Gen 42:21 Then they said to one another, "In truth we are guilty concerning our brother, in that we saw the distress of his soul, when he besought us and we would not listen; therefore, is this distress come upon us."

42:21 καὶ εἶπεν ἕκαστος πρὸς τὸν ἀδελφὸν αὐτοῦ ναί ἐν ἁμαρτίᾳ γάρ ἐσμεν περὶ τοῦ ἀδελφοῦ ἡμῶν ὅτι ὑπερείδομεν τὴν **θλῖψιν** τῆς ψυχῆς αὐτοῦ ὅτε κατεδέετο ἡμῶν καὶ οὐκ εἰσηκούσαμεν αὐτοῦ ἕνεκεν τούτου ἐπῆλθεν ἐφ' ἡμᾶς ἡ **θλῖψις** αὕτη

Acts 7:11 Now **there came** a **famine** throughout all **Egypt** and **Canaan**, and great affliction, and our fathers could find no food[1].

7:11 **ἦλθεν** δὲ **λιμὸς** ἐφ' ὅλην τὴν γῆν **Αἰγύπτου** καὶ **Χανάαν** καὶ θλῖψις μεγάλη καὶ οὐχ εὕρισκον χορτάσματα οἱ πατέρες ἡμῶν

Gen 41:57 Moreover, all the earth came to Egypt to Joseph to buy grain, because the famine was severe over all the earth.

41:57 καὶ πᾶσαι αἱ χῶραι **ἦλθον** εἰς **Αἴγυπτον** ἀγοράζειν πρὸς Ιωσηφ ἐπεκράτησεν γὰρ ὁ **λιμὸς** ἐν πάσῃ τῇ γῇ

---

1. G5527 χόρτασμα hapax in NT, frequent in OT.

JOSEPH

Gen 42:5 Thus, the sons of Israel came to buy among the others who came, for the famine was in the land of Canaan.

42:5 ἦλθον δὲ οἱ υἱοὶ Ισραηλ ἀγοράζειν μετὰ τῶν ἐρχομένων ἦν γὰρ ὁ **λιμὸς** ἐν γῇ Χανααν

In most summaries of the history of Israel, there is little recognition of the history of the people of God outside of Canaan. Nehemiah 9 is an exception.

The phrase "our fathers" πατέρες ἡμῶν occurs in 84 verses of the Greek Scriptures. It appears 9 times in 8 verses of Acts 7[2] and also occurs 5 times in Nehemiah 9[3]. This concentration of "our fathers" in these two chapters allows us to infer that Nehemiah 9 was a source for Acts 7 and basis for the frequent repetition of the phrase "πατέρες ἡμῶν".

Acts 7:12–13 But when Jacob heard that there was grain[4] in Egypt, he sent forth our fathers the first time. (13) And at the second visit Joseph made himself known[5] to his brothers, and Joseph's family became known to Pharaoh.

Luke uses the phrase "made himself known to his brothers" ἀνεγνωρίσθη Ἰωσὴφ τοῖς ἀδελφοῖς αὐτοῦ which appears in Genesis 45:1 as follows: Ιωσηφ ἡνίκα ἀνεγνωρίζετο τοῖς ἀδελφοῖς αὐτοῦ.

The famine was of sufficient length to necessitate two trips to Egypt. According to Luke, "in salvation history God will favor or visit his people and they will not recognize it. When God 'visits' them a second time, they can no longer claim ignorance."[6]

Acts 7:14 And Joseph sent and called[7] to him Jacob his father and all his kindred, seventy-five[8] souls;

2. Verses 11, 12, 15, 19, 38, 39, 44, 45.
3. Verses 9, 16, 32, 34, 36.
4. G6079 σιτίον LXX none; Acts 7:12
5. G319 ἀναγνωρίζω LXX Gen 45:1; Acts 7:13; double hapax.
6. Witherington, 268.
7. G3333 μετακαλέω LXX Hosea 11:1,2; Acts 7:14; 10:32; 20:17; 24:25.
8. ἑβδομήκοντα πέντε seventy-five; Fitzmyer, Dead Sea, 7, fn18.

Acts 7:14 ἀποστείλας δὲ Ἰωσὴφ, μετεκαλέσατο Ἰακὼβ, τὸν πατέρα αὐτοῦ, καὶ πᾶσαν τὴν συγγένειαν, ἐν ψυχαῖς ἑβδομήκοντα πέντε.

Both Genesis 46:27 (MT) and (SP); Ex 1:5; Dt 10:22 sets the figure at 70 (i.e. 66 plus Jacob, Joseph and the latter's two sons). Josephus, *Ant.* 2:176 and The Book of Jubilees 44:33 agree. In Ex 1:5 the Hebrew Qumran fragment 4QExod-b 1.5(DJD 12.18,84) says 75 as does the LXX of Gen 46:27 and Ex 1:5 but giving Joseph 9 sons instead of the two of MT (Gen. 46:27) Acts 7:15-16 and Jacob went down into Egypt. And he died, himself and our fathers, (16) and they were carried back to Shechem and laid in the tomb that Abraham had bought[9] for a sum of silver from the sons of Hamor in Shechem.

Acts 7:15 Καὶ κατέβη Ἰακὼβ εἰς Αἴγυπτον καὶ ἐτελεύτησεν, αὐτὸς καὶ οἱ πατέρες ἡμῶν,

Acts 7:16 καὶ μετετέθησαν εἰς Συχὲμ καὶ ἐτέθησαν ἐν τῷ μνήματι ᾧ ὠνήσατο Ἀβραὰμ τιμῆς ἀργυρίου παρὰ τῶν υἱῶν Ἐμμὼρ ἐν Συχὲμ.

Johnson has indicated that Luke has "either confused these traditions, or telescoped them into one."[10] There are four additional possibilities:

1. Stephen meant to say Jacob rather than Abraham which would agree with Gen 33:19; Joshua 24:32; Josephus, Antiquities 2:199-200 and the Book of Jubilees 45:15; 46:9-10;
2. 2). It is not unusual for the family to discover after burying a relative that the decedent had previously purchased a lot in another cemetery;
3. Shulam has suggested that Joseph had instructed that he be buried in the same neighborhood from which he had been kidnapped, Shechem;[11] and

---

9. G5608 ὠνέομαι LXX none; M & M, 701; Acts 7:16
10. Johnson, 119.
11. Shulam, 348.

4. Stephen employed hidden polemics. This seems likely since Stephen has alluded to Jos 24:32 which includes the phrase "sons of Israel" in the sentence "The bones of Joseph which the sons of Israel brought up from Egypt were buried at Shechem...."

Jub. 46:8–9 and Ant. 2.199 both say Joseph's brothers are buried in Hebron.

Chapter 6

Moses

Acts 7:17 "But as the time of the promise drew near, which God had granted to Abraham, the people grew and multiplied in Egypt.

7:17 Καθὼς δὲ ἤγγιζεν ὁ χρόνος τῆς ἐπαγγελίας ἧς ὤμοσεν ὁ θεὸς τῷ Ἀβραάμ **ηὔξησεν** ὁ λαὸς **καὶ ἐπληθύνθη** ἐν Αἰγύπτῳ

Ex 1:7 But the descendants of Israel were fruitful and increased greatly; they multiplied and grew exceedingly strong; so that the land was filled with them

Ex 1:7 οἱ δὲ υἱοὶ Ισραηλ **ηὐξήθησαν καὶ ἐπληθύνθησαν** καὶ χυδαῖοι ἐγένοντο καὶ κατίσχυον σφόδρα σφόδρα ἐπλήθυνεν δὲ ἡ γῆ αὐτούς

THIS verse is based upon Exodus 1:7 and is a reminder that in Acts 6:1 they "were increasing in numbers" like the people in Egypt. While the RSV translation has "the descendants of Israel, both the SP and the MT have "the sons of Israel."

Tannehill notes that the second reference to Ex 1:7–8 appears in Acts in verse 17 and is further evidence of its influence in Acts.[1] Clearly Luke intends to make a comparison between

---

1. Tannehill, 82.

MOSES

the growth of the Jesus movement and the situation in Israel in Exodus. None of the commentators have noticed that Stephen has also alluded to the "υἱοὶ Ἰσραηλ" sons of Israel.

Acts 7:18 till there arose over Egypt another king who had not known Joseph.

The bold type clearly indicates that Stephen borrowed this phrase from Exodus 1:8.

7:18 ἄχρις οὗ ἀνέστη βασιλεὺς ἕτερος ὃς οὐκ ᾔδει τὸν Ἰωσήφ

> Exodus 1:8 (RSV) Now there arose a new king over Egypt, who did not know Joseph.

> Ex 1:8 ἀνέστη δὲ βασιλεὺς ἕτερος ἐπ' Αἴγυπτον ὃς οὐκ ᾔδει τὸν Ιωσηφ

Acts 7:19 He dealt craftily[2] with our race and forced our fathers to expose[3] their infants, that they might not be kept alive.[4]

Verse 19 is based upon Exod 1:10-22. Only the verb ζῳογονέω is borrowed from Exod 1:17, 22.

Acts 7:20 At this time Moses was born, and was beautiful[5] before God. And he was brought[6] up for three months in his father's house;

> 7:20 ἐν ᾧ καιρῷ ἐγεννήθη Μωσῆς, καὶ ἦν ἀστεῖος τῷ θεῷ ὃς ἀνετράφη **μῆνας τρεῖς** ἐν τῷ οἴκῳ τοῦ πατρός αὐτοῦ

> Ex 2:2 The woman conceived and bore a son; and when she saw that he was a goodly child, she hid him three months.

> 2:2 καὶ ἐν γαστρὶ ἔλαβεν καὶ ἔτεκεν ἄρσεν ἰδόντες δὲ αὐτὸ ἀστεῖον ἐσκέπασαν αὐτὸ **μῆνας τρεῖς**

---

2. G2686 κατασοφίζομαι is a double hapax; Ex 1:10; Acts 7:19.
3. G1570 ἔκθετος LXX none; M & M, 194; Acts 7:19.
4. G2225 ζῳογονέω LXX numerous; Lk 17:33; Acts 7:19; 1 Ti 6:13.
5. G791 ἀστεῖος LXX Ex 2:2; Nm 22:32; Acts 7:20; Heb 11:23.
6. G397 ἀνατρέφω LXX none; Acts 7:20, 21; 22:3.

The brief biographical of Moses: birth (v.20), forced exposure (v.21a), adoption (v.21b) and education summarizes Ex 2:2–10. The only summaries providing more space to Moses are Sir 44:23– 45:5; 2 Bar 59:1–12; 1 En 89:16–38.

Using Moses, the prophet, as a model, Luke composes the history of the rejections of God's messengers by the people. "Stephen's speech, in particular his portrait of Moses, most clearly establishes the prophetic pattern found throughout Luke-Acts."[7]

> Acts 7:21 and when he was exposed,[8] Pharaoh's daughter adopted him and brought him up as her own son.
>
> 7:21 ἐκτεθέντα δὲ αὐτὸν ἀνείλετο αὐτὸν ἡ θυγάτηρ Φαραὼ καὶ ἀνεθρέψατο αὐτόν ἑαυτῇ εἰς υἱόν

"Pharaoh's daughter took him" is from LXX Ex 2:5 while "raised him as her own son" is from Ex 2:10.

> Acts 7:22 And Moses was instructed in all the wisdom of the Egyptians, and he was mighty in his words and deeds.
>
> Acts 7:22 καὶ ἐπαιδεύθη Μωϋσῆς [ἐν] πάσῃ σοφίᾳ Αἰγυπτίων; ἦν δὲ δυνατὸς ἐν λόγοις καὶ ἔργοις αὐτοῦ.

The phrase "wonders and signs" occurs 4 times in the RSV but only in Acts[9]. The more common phrase "signs and wonders" appears 30 times in the RSV including 4 times in Acts[10].

In verses 20–22, "instructed in all Egyptian wisdom" follows the classic biographical triad of birth, nurture, education. The phrase "mighty in his words and deeds" (δυνατὸς ἐν λόγοις καὶ ἐν ἔργοις) is not in Exodus but the wording does echo Luke 24:19 where Luke describes Jesus as προφήτης δυνατὸς ἐν ἔργῳ καὶ λόγῳ.

Stephen's speech in this verse not only establishes a close relationship between Moses and Jesus not given to any other prophet

---

7. Shepherd, Narrative Function of the Holy Spirit, 177.
8. G1620 ἐκτίθημι LXX numerous, Acts 7:21; 11:4; 18:26; 28:23.
9. Verses 2:22; 2:43; 6:8; 7:36
10. Verses 4:30; 5:12; 14:3; 15:12.

but also the words of Deut. 18:15 and verse 7:37 follows the "signs and wonders" of 7:36 and prepare for the "living words" of 7:38.

> Acts 7:23 "When he was forty years old, it came into his heart to visit his brethren, the sons of Israel.
>
> Acts 7:23 Ὡς δὲ ἐπληροῦτο αὐτῷ τεσσερακονταέτης χρόνος, ἀνέβη ἐπὶ τὴν καρδίαν αὐτοῦ ἐπισκέψασθαι τοὺς ἀδελφοὺς αὐτοῦ, τοὺς υἱοὺς Ἰσραήλ.

The manner of referring to the Israelites υἱοὺς Ἰσραήλ, "the sons of Israel" occurs in speeches in 7:23, 37; 10:36. The Prophet, Jeremiah (6th century BCE) is the first to distinguish the "sons of Israel" from the "sons of Judah."[11]

Jer 32:30 For the sons of Israel and the sons of Judah have done nothing but evil in my sight from their youth; the sons of Israel have done nothing but provoke me to anger by the work of their hands, says the LORD.

Jer 32:32 because of all the evil of the sons of Israel and the sons of Judah which they did to provoke me to anger--their kings and their princes, their priests and their prophets, the men of Judah and the inhabitants of Jerusalem.

The first clear mention of Samaritans as a distinctive group is in the book of Ecclesiasticus (50:25), which dates from around 180 BCE. There was no overt anti-Shechemite polemic until we reach Ecclesiasticus 50:26 with the doubtful exception of Hosea 6:9.

The Samaritans were rejected by the Jews in the intertestamental period. Ecclesiasticus 50:25–26 speaks of them as "no nation" and as "the foolish people that dwell in Shechem." The Testament of Levi also calls Shechem "a city of fools." This derogation is relevant to understanding John 8:48, for the Jews called Jesus a Samaritan.

The meanings of the "sons of Israel" and the "Hebrews" is the heart of the argument but also the crux and stumbling block. The question of the ethnic identity of Stephen, who is presumed to be a Hellenist because he, like the other six appointed to wait on tables, has a Greek name, is unknown. Incidentally, with respect

---

11. Jer. 32:30 (RSV).

to Greek names, based on the papyri, at least three-fourths of the Egyptian Jews had Greek names, rather than Hebrew.[12] J. N. Sevenster, after extensive work on the inscriptional evidence of first-century Judaism, describes the dominance extensive work on the inscriptional evidence of first-century Judaism, describes the dominance of Greek among the western Diaspora notes that . . . "by far the majority of the Diaspora Jews who went on pilgrimage to Jerusalem or settled in the Jewish land spoke Greek."[13] Luke has not implicitly identified Stephen as a Hebrew or Hellenist. "The majority of scholars, however, do consider Stephen to have been a Hellenist, whatever that designation may imply."[14] Todd Penner has commented that "Despite the relative lack of clues, speculation has not been muted as a result."[15] "Esler . . . goes to great length to demonstrate that the 'Hellenists' spoke Greek and the 'Hebrews' spoke Aramaic."[16]

Samaritans called themselves Hebrews from the third century BCE as confirmed by Josephus[17] retaining the name originally given to the people of the twelve tribes (Gen. 39:14; 40:15; Ex. 2:7; 3:18; 3:18; 5:3; 1 Sam 4:6, 9, etc.) based on their spoken language. Stefan Schorch states:

> SH [Samaritan Hebrew], as it is heard in the reading of the Torah among the Samaritan community until our days, originates in the late Second Temple period and was the language spoken among the (proto-) Samaritans in the late second century BCE. SH is a Hebrew dialect of its own, distinct from both the Hebrew dialect as preserved in Tiberian Hebrew pronunciation of the Bible and from Mishnaic Hebrew.[18]

---

12. Stefon, Judaism: History, Belief, and Practice, 40.
13. Sevenster, Do You Know Greek?, 82.
14. Hill, Hellenists and Hebrews, 46.
15. Penner, In Praise of Christian Origins, 71.
16. Penner citing Esler, Community and Gospel, 141–3.
17. Ant. 11.334.
18. Schorch, Spoken Hebrew of Late Second Temple Period, 190–1.

Knoppers makes the interesting observation that "diplomatic correspondence was written in Aramaic (Erza 4:8–16, 17–22; 5:7–17; 6:2–5, 6–12), especially with respect to regional Achaemenid authorities . . . and that all of Sanballat are recorded or cited in Hebrew (Neh. 2:20' 6:3, 4, 8–9)."[19] Knoppers also notes that Nehemiah does "complain about the children of Judean mixed marriages speaking other tongues, such as Ashdodite, and not knowing how to speak Juhahite (Yehudit; Neh. 13:23)." "From his perspective, sharing a common language was a priority in maintaining a distinct community. Having a common language was evidently a problem for the offspring of the connubials with the Moabites, Ammonites, and Ashdodites, but ironically not a problem for the governors of Samaria and Judah.[20]

Several scholars have recognized that the prologue to the Greek version of Sirach offers valuable insight to the spoken language of its day. "The social context is one in which the grandson is translating for a Greek speaking audience, which mostly likely does not know Hebrew, at least not enough to read his grandfather's book."[21] In short, most Judeans were no longer communicating in Hebrew and thus would not be included in the group identified as "Hebrews" by the author of Acts 6.

The Samaritans proudly say we are *shamerim*שֹׁמְרִים,Keepers [of the Law]," rather than *shomronim*, Samaritans, derived from the geographical designation, as the Jews know them. They consider themselves *Bnei Yisrael* ("Sons of Israel" or "Israelites"), belonging to the kingdom of the ten tribes, but do not regard themselves to be *Yehudim* (Jews).

The audience has been prepared by step progression for the allusion to υἱοὺς Ἰσραήλ, ("the sons of Israel") in Lev. Step progression with the respect to "the sons of Israel" begins with an extremely subtle allusion in verse 6:1 in the use of the word γογγυσμός directing attention to the murmuring alluded to in Exodus 16:7, 8*,9, 12. Verses 9–10 state: And Moses said to Aaron, "Say to the

19. Knoppers, Nehemiah and Sanballat, 328–329.
20. Knoppers, 329.
21. Benjamin, Translation Greek in Sirach, 78.

whole congregation of the sons of Israel, 'Come near before the LORD, for He has heard your murmurings.'" And as Aaron spoke to the whole congregation of **the sons of Israel**, they looked toward the wilderness, and behold, the glory of the LORD appeared in the cloud. The next step in the progression occurs in Stephen's speech in 7:23, 37 which both include υἱοὺς 'Ισραήλ, ("the sons of Israel") (emphasis added).

> Acts 7:24 And seeing one of them being wronged, he defended[22] the oppressed[23] man and avenged him by striking the Egyptian.
>
> 7:24 καὶ ἰδών τινα ἀδικούμενον ἠμύνατο καὶ ἐποίησεν ἐκδίκησιν τῷ καταπονουμένῳ πατάξας τὸν Αἰγύπτιον

In the LXX of Ex 2:11, Moses asked: "why are you beating your neighbor?" The phrase "striking down the Egyptian" (πατάξας τὸν Αἰγύπτιον) is taken from Ex 2:12. Moses is depicted as a champion of justice (ἐκδίκησις) for the oppressed.

> Acts 7:25 He supposed that his brethren understood that God was giving them deliverance by his hand, but they did not understand.
>
> Acts 7:25 ἐνόμιζεν δὲ συνιέναι τοὺς ἀδελφοὺς [αὐτοῦ] ὅτι ὁ Θεὸς διὰ χειρὸς αὐτοῦ δίδωσιν σωτηρίαν αὐτοῖς, οἱ δὲ οὐ συνῆκαν.

A disobedient, stiff-necked people does not understand God's deliverance through his agent, Moses or Jesus.

The theme "they did not understand" does not appear in Exodus or any of the retellings of the Moses story but it is an important theme in the Gospel of Luke. Mary believes the message of the Angel Gabriel but twelve years later, when she and her husband find Jesus in the Temple, "they did not understand." The two Temple stories of the priest Zechariah and the boy Jesus stand by themselves yet frame the four pairs of stories in between about lack of understanding. Yet, throughout the complex narrative Luke

---

22. G292 ἀμύνομαι LXX, several, Acts 7:24.
23. G2669 καταπονέω LXX none; M & M 331; Acts 7:24; 2 Pe 2:7.

provides clues so that Theophilus might understand. This lack of understanding appears throughout the Gospel [2:50; 8:10; 18:34 and 24:45; Acts 7:25; 28:26–27], and is an important theme in the presentation to Theophilus. These passages are directed to most excellent Theophilus.

Luke uses ἐνόμιζεν to denote an assumption wrongly made that leads persons to act as if it were true. See also Lk. 2:44; Acts 8:20, 14:19; 21:29.[24]

> Acts 7:26 And on the following day he appeared to them as they were quarreling and would have reconciled[25] them, saying, 'Men, you are brethren, why do you wrong each other?'
>
> Acts 7:26 Τῇ τε ἐπιούσῃ ἡμέρᾳ, ὤφθη αὐτοῖς μαχομένοις καὶ συνήλλασσεν αὐτοὺς εἰς εἰρήνην, εἰπών, Ἄνδρες, ἀδελφοί ἐστε ἵνα τί ἀδικεῖτε ἀλλήλους ?

Moses tried to make peace between two quarrelling men. The theme of peace is associated with the ministry of Jesus. This verse creates another comparison between Moses and Jesus (Luke 1:79; 2:14, 29; Acts 10:36).

> Acts 7:27–28 But the man who was wronging his neighbor thrust him aside, saying, 'Who made you a ruler and a judge over us? (28) Do you want to kill me as you killed the Egyptian yesterday?'
>
> 7:27 ὁ δὲ ἀδικῶν τὸν πλησίον ἀπώσατο αὐτὸν εἰπών Τίς σε κατέστησεν ἄρχοντα καὶ δικαστὴν ἐφ' ἡμᾶς 28 μὴ ἀνελεῖν με σὺ θέλεις ὃν τρόπον ἀνεῖλες ἐχθὲς τὸν Αἰγύπτιον
>
> Ex 2:14 He answered, "Who made you a prince and a judge over us? Do you mean to kill me as you killed the Egyptian?" Then Moses was afraid, and thought, "Surely the thing is known."

---

24. G3543; Green, The Theology of the Gospel of Luke, 57 fn 13.
25. G4900 συναλλάσσω LXX none; M & M, 602; Acts 7:26, hapax.

2:14 ὁ δὲ εἶπεν τίς σε κατέστησεν **ἄρχοντα καὶ δικαστὴν ἐφ' ἡμῶν μὴ ἀνελεῖν με** σὺ θέλεις ὃν τρόπον ἀνεῖλες ἐχθὲς **τὸν Αἰγύπτιον** ἐφοβήθη δὲ Μωυσῆς καὶ εἶπεν εἰ οὕτως ἐμφανὲς γέγονεν τὸ ῥῆμα τοῦτο

The bold type shows what Greek words are in both Acts 7:27–28 and Ex 2:14 suggesting that Ex 2:14 was utilized as a source.

> Acts 7:29 At this retort Moses fled, and became an exile (πάροικος) in the land of Mid'ian, where he became the father of two sons.

> 7:29 ἔφυγεν Μωϋσῆς ἐν τῷ λόγῳ τούτῳ, καὶ ἐγένετο πάροικος ἐν γῇ Μαδιάμ, οὗ ἐγέννησεν υἱοὺς δύο.

The phrase "ἐν τῷ λόγῳ" literally means "at this word." In Ex 2:14, Moses is fearful that the Pharaoh would "hear this word." In Ex 2:22, we read Moses "named his first son Gershom; for he said, 'I have been a sojourner πάροικός in a foreign land.'"

> Acts 7:30 "Now when forty years had passed, an angel appeared to him in the wilderness of Mount Sinai, in a flame of fire in a bush.

> Acts 7:30 Καὶ πληρωθέντων ἐτῶν τεσσαράκοντα ὤφθη αὐτῷ ἐν τῇ ἐρήμῳ τοῦ ὄρους Σινᾶ ἄγγελος Κυρίου ἐν φλογὶ πυρὸς βάτου

It is appropriate that the burning bush incident takes place near Mount Sinai where Moses was named by God to lead the Israelites out of Egypt. Sinai is a mountain described in Exodus 19:18 as being on fire.

According to Jub. 1:27, 29; 2:1 "The Angel of Presence talked with Moses on Mount Sinai.

Exo 3:1 Now Moses was keeping the flock of his father-in-law, Jethro, the priest of Mid'ian; and he led his flock to the west side of the wilderness, and came to Horeb, the mountain of God.

> Exo 3:2 And the angel of the LORD appeared to him in a flame of fire out of the midst of a bush; and he looked, and lo, the bush was burning, yet it was not consumed.

Moses

3:1 καὶ Μωυσῆς ἦν ποιμαίνων τὰ πρόβατα Ιοθορ τοῦ γαμβροῦ αὐτοῦ τοῦ ἱερέως Μαδιαμ καὶ ἤγαγεν τὰ πρόβατα ὑπὸ τὴν **ἔρημον** καὶ ἦλθεν εἰς τὸ ὄρος Χωρηβ

3:2 ὤφθη δὲ **αὐτῷ ἄγγελος κυρίου ἐν φλογὶ πυρὸς ἐκ τοῦ βάτου** καὶ ὁρᾷ ὅτι ὁ βάτος καίεται πυρί ὁ δὲ βάτος οὐ κατεκαίετο

The bold type shows what Greek words are in Acts 7:30 and Ex 3:2 suggesting that Ex 3:2 was used as a source.

The idea of explicitly sacred space is encountered for the first time with the fire in the bush incident.

> Acts 7:31–32 When Moses saw it, he wondered at the sight; and as he drew near to look, the voice of the LORD came, (32) 'I am the God of your fathers, the God of Abraham and of Isaac and of Jacob.' And Moses trembled and did not dare to look.

7:31 ὁ δὲ Μωσῆς ἰδὼν ἐθαύμασεν τὸ ὅραμα προσερχομένου δὲ αὐτοῦ κατανοῆσαι ἐγένετο φωνὴ κυρίου πρὸς αὐτόν,

7:32 Ἐγὼ ὁ θεὸς τῶν πατέρων σου ὁ **θεὸς Ἀβραὰμ καὶ ὁ Θεὸς Ἰσαὰκ καὶ ὁ Θεὸς Ἰακώβ** ἔντρομος δὲ γενόμενος Μωσῆς οὐκ ἐτόλμα κατανοῆσαι

Exo 3:6 MT And he said, "I am the God of your father, the God of Abraham, the God of Isaac, and the God of Jacob." And Moses hid his face, for he was afraid to look at God.

3:6 καὶ εἶπεν αὐτῷ ἐγώ εἰμι ὁ θεὸς τοῦ πατρός σου **θεὸς Αβρααμ καὶ θεὸς Ισαακ καὶ θεὸς Ιακωβ** ἀπέστρεψεν δὲ Μωυσῆς τὸ πρόσωπον αὐτοῦ εὐλαβεῖτο γὰρ κατεμβλέψαι ἐνώπιον τοῦ θεοῦ

> Acts 7:33 And the LORD said to him, 'Take off the shoes from your feet, for the place where you are standing is holy ground.

7:33 εἶπεν δὲ αὐτῷ ὁ κύριος Λῦσον τὸ ὑπόδημα **τῶν ποδῶν σου** ὁ γὰρ τόπος ἐν ᾧ ἕστηκας γῆ ἁγία ἐστίν

Ex 3:5 Then he said, "Do not come near; put off your shoes from your feet, for the place on which you are standing is holy ground."

3:5 καὶ εἶπεν μὴ ἐγγίσῃς ὧδε λῦσαι τὸ ὑπόδημα ἐκ τῶν ποδῶν σου ὁ γὰρ τόπος ἐν ᾧ σὺ ἕστηκας γῆ ἁγία ἐστίν

Verse 33 with its directive "Take off the shoes from your feet, for the place where you are standing is holy ground" more accurately expresses the viewpoint of Stephen. This spot was only holy because the LORD was speaking to Moses. This spot lost its holiness when the theophany of the burning bush concluded. As Nahum Sarna stated: "It is solely the theophany that temporarily imparts sanctity to the site, rendering it inaccessible to man."[26]

Acts 7:34 I have surely seen the ill-treatment[27] of my people that are in Egypt and heard their groaning, and I have come down to deliver them. And now come, I will send you to Egypt.'

7:34 ἰδὼν εἶδον τὴν κάκωσιν τοῦ λαοῦ μου τοῦ ἐν Αἰγύπτῳ καὶ τοῦ στεναγμοῦ αὐτῶν ἤκουσα καὶ κατέβην ἐξελέσθαι αὐτούς καὶ νῦν δεῦρο ἀποστέλω σε εἰς Αἴγυπτον

Ex 3:7 Then the LORD said, "I have seen the affliction of my people who are in Egypt, and have heard their cry because of their taskmasters; I know their sufferings,

Ex 3:7 εἶπεν δὲ κύριος πρὸς Μωυσῆν ἰδὼν εἶδον τὴν κάκωσιν τοῦ λαοῦ μου τοῦ ἐν Waiting on Tables

Αἰγύπτῳ καὶ τῆς κραυγῆς αὐτῶν ἀκήκοα ἀπὸ τῶν ἐργοδιωκτῶν οἶδα γὰρ τὴν ὀδύνην αὐτῶν

Acts 7:35 "This Moses whom they refused, saying, 'Who made you a ruler and a judge?' God sent as both ruler and deliverer[28] by the hand of the angel that appeared to him in the bush.

---

26. Sarna, JPS Torah Commentary on Exodus, 15.
27. G2561 κάκωσις Ex 3:7,17; Job 31:29[Symm.]; Acts 7:34.
28. G3086 λυτρωτής Lev 25:31,32; Acts 7:35.

MOSES

Acts 7:35 Τοῦτον τὸν Μωϋσῆν, ὃν ἠρνήσαντο, εἰπόντες, Τίς σε κατέστησεν ἄρχοντα καὶ δικαστήν ;

The phrase "appeared to him in the bush" (ὀφθέντος αὐτῷ ἐν τῇ βάτῳ) is found in Deut 33:16 (ὀφθέντι ἐν τῷ βάτῳ).

To speak of Moses as a deliverer is a rebuttal of the accusation against Stephen in Acts 6:11, 14.[29]

Verse 35 is an abrupt change of the style of the speech from narrative to declarative statements marked using the Greek demonstrative pronoun οὗτος and threefold use of demonstrative pronoun οὗτός in verses 36–38 employed in praise of Moses. Johnson has noted that "The form of this first declaration is particularly interesting, for it matches precisely the 'kergmatic' statement of Jesus' rejection and vindication in Acts 3:13–15, ..."[30] Beginning with verse 35, this retelling by Stephen is unlike any prior retellings of the Moses story. It "has no parallel in the Jewish versions of Moses story."[31]

The focus on Moses in Acts 7 is unprecedented but explainable in that Moses is an important person in Samaritan theology. The origins of Samaritan ideas about Moses are based on Deut. 32–34. "Not only will there be no other prophet like him (Deut. 34.10), but heaven and earth were obedient to him."[32]

> Acts 7:36 He led them out, having performed wonders and signs in Egypt and at the Red Sea, and in the wilderness for forty years.
>
> 7:36 οὗτος ἐξήγαγεν αὐτοὺς ποιήσας τέρατα καὶ σημεῖα ἐν γῇ Αἰγύπτῳ καὶ ἐν
>
> Ἐρυθρᾷ Θαλάσσῃ καὶ ἐν τῇ ἐρήμῳ ἔτη τεσσεράκοντα
>
> Deu 34:11 none like him for all the signs and the wonders which the LORD sent him to do in the land of Egypt, to Pharaoh and to all his servants and to all his land,

---

29. Barrett, 364 citing Bauernfeind, 110.
30. Johnson, 129.
31. Johnson, 129.
32. MacDonald, Theology, 149.

34:11 ἐν πᾶσι τοῖς **σημείοις καὶ τέρασιν** ὃν ἀπέστειλεν αὐτὸν κύριος ποιῆσαι αὐτὰ **ἐν γῇ Αἰγύπτῳ** Φαραω καὶ τοῖς θεράπουσιν αὐτοῦ καὶ πάσῃ τῇ γῇ αὐτοῦ

Stephen summarizes the events of the exodus focusing on the role of Moses in the land of Egypt, at the Red Sea and in the wilderness demonstrating "that the prophetic power was active throughout Moses' ministry among the people."[33]

Acts 7:37 This is the Moses who said to the **sons of Israel**, God will raise up for you a prophet from your brethren as he raised me up.

Stephen appears to cite the same text as Peter in Acts 3:22 but nonetheless makes the same point by implying that Jesus is the fulfillment of Moses' prophecy.

7:37 οὗτός ἐστιν ὁ Μωϋσῆς ὁ εἰπὼν τοῖς **υἱοῖς Ἰσραήλ** Προφήτην ὑμῖν ἀναστήσει Κύριος ὁ θεὸς ὑμῶν ἐκ τῶν ἀδελφῶν ὑμῶν ὡς ἐμέ **αὐτοῦ ἀκούσεσθε**

Deut 18:15 "The LORD your God will raise up for you a prophet like me from among you, from your brethren--him you shall heed-

18:15 **προφήτην ἐκ τῶν ἀδελφῶν** σου ὡς ἐμὲ ἀναστήσει σοι **κύριος ὁ θεός σου αὐτοῦ ἀκούσεσθε**

The Samaritan Pentateuch was known to some of the Church Fathers such as Eusebius (265–340) and Jerome (340–420) but until the discovery of the Dead Sea Scrolls its antiquity had been in question. The most important variants are the ones which reveal the fundamental points at issue between the Samaritans and Jews. The Samaritans emphasized the importance of Shechem and Mount Gerizim and declared that God had chosen them to be the center of the nation. Thus, where Moses in Deuteronomy 12:5 and other places, speaks of "the place which the LORD your God shall choose" (later identified as Jerusalem), the Samaritan edition translates it "the place which the LORD your God has chosen" - meaning Mount Gerizim, which has already been specified

---

33. Johnson, 129.

in Deuteronomy 27:4-8 where Moses commands that the stones bearing the words of the Law and an altar of unknown stones are to be set up on Mount Ebal, the Samaritan text has Gerizim for Ebal.

Exodus lies at the center of the Judeo-Christian tradition. Thus, the most important difference occurs in Chapter 20, which contains the extraordinary 10th Commandment, reads as follows (translation of the SP provided by Moses Gaster, 1923):

> And it shall come to pass when the LORD thy God will bring thee into the land of the Canaanites whither thou goest to take possession of it, thou shalt erect unto thee large stones, and thou shalt cover them with lime, and thou shalt write upon the stones all the words of this Law, and it shall come to pass when ye cross the Jordan, ye shall erect these stones which I command thee upon Mount Gerizim, and thou shalt build there an altar unto the LORD thy God, an altar of stones, and thou shalt not lift upon them iron, of perfect stones shalt thou build thine altar, and thou shalt bring upon it burnt offerings to the LORD thy God, and thou shalt sacrifice peace offerings, and thou shalt eat there and rejoice before the LORD thy God. That mountain is on the other side of the Jordan at the end of the road towards the going down of the sun in the land of the Canaanites who dwell in the Arabah facing Gilgal close by Elon Moreh facing Shechem.

Exodus 20 of the SP at three points includes material not found in the MT. At the first point, Exodus 20:17 includes Ex 13:11a; Deut 27:2b-3a; 27:4-7; and Deut 11:30. The second one in Deut 20:19 includes Deut 5:24-27. The third point at Exodus 20:22a includes 5:28b-29; 18:18-22 and 5:30-31. The third instance with the same order of verses can be found in several different fragments from Qumran. The Qumran material clarified the eschatological function of the prophet like Moses.

According to Dillon, "Stephen's sequential Exodus citations – (including Ex 20:17f, SP – represents a single author, and from what we have seen inclines us to agree that is *not* St. Luke."[34]

In verse 37, Stephen appears to quote Deuteronomy 18:15 by including a saying about God raising up a prophet like Moses. Luke had essentially been following Genesis and Exodus (up to and including Acts 7:34). Thus Deuteronomy 18:15 is out of place and furthermore, Exodus 20 of the SP would not be out of place. SP Exodus 20 included what is called the Samaritan tenth commandment, established Mount Gerizim as the sacred place that God has chosen. Stephen must have been following the Samaritan Pentateuch.

Scharlemann noted: "That is to say, Stephen quotes the passage as it is found in Exodus 20:21b of the Samaritan Pentateuch, at a point immediately after the account of the giving of the law on Mount Sinai. . . ."[35] There can be little doubt, therefore, that Stephen is here echoing a Samaritan context dealing with the revelation on Mount Sinai. We must add here the notice that certain fragments of a Samaritan recension were found among the Dead Sea Scrolls. They contain the same kind of transposition as we have noted, including the expansion at Exodus 20:21."[36]

In fact, Stephen in verse 37, quoted the SP. As noted earlier, Schorch demonstrated conclusively that the Samaritan version of Deuteronomy is the original and it was modified by the Judeans of the southern kingdom, proving that the victors rewrite history and sacred scripture.

Stephen is referring to the promise made in the Wilderness of the coming of a faithful eschatological prophet. A prophet like Moses was envisioned by the Qumran writers. Biblical support for this figure is preserved in the citation of Deut 18:18–19 found in 4QTestimonia (4Q175 1.5–8) and The Community Rule (IQS 9:10–11; also, IQS 1.1–3). The phrase "until a faithful prophet

---

34. Dillon, 236.
35. Scharlemann, *Stephen*, 46.
36. Scharlemann, *Stephen*, 46.

should arise" in 1 Macc 1:41 borrows images of faithful prophet from Num 12:7 and ideal prophet from Deut 34:10.

This explanation about the apparent out-of-place insertion was first made by Paul Kahle in 1915.[37]

Furthermore, it should be noted that the Samaritans rely upon two verses that have not been cited in the discussions about verse 37 which in the SP and MT are in substantial agreement: Deut. 34:10 SP "And since that time no prophet has risen in Israel like Moses" and Deut. 4:2 SP "You shall not add to the word which I am commanding you today, nor take away from it." The Samaritans rely on the first verse to reject the prophets that followed Moses and the second verse to reject the changes made by the Judeans as having no scriptural basis.

Finally, the phrase "sons of Israel" makes its second appearance in Stephen's speech and does so in a verse clearly directing our attention to the SP. None of the commentators discuss the significance of this phrase.

> Acts 7:38 This is he who was in the congregation in the wilderness with the angel who spoke to him at Mount Sinai, and with our fathers; and he received living oracles to give to us.
>
> Acts 7:38 οὗτός ἐστιν ὁ γενόμενος ἐν τῇ ἐκκλησίᾳ ἐν τῇ ἐρήμῳ, μετὰ τοῦ ἀγγέλου τοῦ λαλοῦντος αὐτῷ ἐν τῷ ὄρει Σινᾶ, καὶ τῶν πατέρων ἡμῶν, ὃς ἐδέξατο λόγια ζῶντα δοῦναι ἡμῖν,

Although there is no detailed discussion of the law, it is recognized as "living oracles" of divine origin (7:38). "The phrase "living words/oracles" does not appear in the LXX, but the connection between law and life is constantly drawn (e.g., Deut. 4:1,33; 5:26; 16:20; 30:15; 32:45; also LXX Ps. 118:25, 50, 154)."[38] Moses received living oracles, the very word of God to convey to the people of God.

---

37. Scroggs, "The Earliest Hellenistic Community," 176–206.
38. Johnson, *Sacra Pagina*, Acts, 130.

The living oracles in Acts refer specifically to the Ten Commandments, more broadly to the Torah, which were to be given to us. But it should be noted, the Samaritans have their own version of the Ten Commandments and consequently their own view of "living oracles."

Verses 35–38 refute the charges (6.11) that Stephen spoke against Moses. In fact, Stephen praised him as a ruler, deliverer, one who spoke with the angel, miracle worker, prophet and receiver of Living words, Torah.

> Acts 7:39 Our fathers refused to obey him, but thrust him aside, and in their hearts, they turned[39] to Egypt,
>
> 7:39 ᾧ οὐκ ἠθέλησαν ὑπήκοοι γενέσθαι οἱ πατέρες ἡμῶν ἀλλ' ἀπώσαντο καὶ **στράφησαν** ταῖς καρδίαις αὐτῶν **εἰς Αἴγυπτον**
>
> Num 14:3 Why does the LORD bring us into this land, to fall by the sword? Our wives and our little ones our little ones will become a prey; would it not be better for us to go back to Egypt?"
>
> 14:3 καὶ ἵνα τί κύριος εἰσάγει ἡμᾶς εἰς τὴν γῆν ταύτην πεσεῖν ἐν πολέμῳ αἱ γυναῖκες ἡμῶν καὶ τὰ παιδία ἔσονται εἰς διαρπαγήν νῦν οὖν βέλτιον ἡμῖν ἐστιν **ἀποστραφῆναι εἰς Αἴγυπτον**

Krodel has noted "The rejection of God's agent inevitably leads to idolatry, ..."[40]

Acts 7:39 makes clear that Israel's worship of the golden calf at Sinai was a continuation of the idolatry they began to commit in Egypt. Ezekiel 23:27 confirms that they brought their idolatrous "harlotry brought from the land of Egypt."

This regular pattern of prophetic rejection is important for understanding Stephen's speech. As a group the Jewish people depicted have repudiated God's word: 1 Sam. 12:22; Psalm 61:5; 76:8; 76:8; 77:60,67 LXX; Jer. 23:17; Acts 7:27, 39.

---

39. G4762 ἐστράφησαν
40. Krodel, 147.

MOSES

"The figure of Moses dominates the speech" and "20 of the 50 verses concern Moses."[41] This impressive presentation is part of the step progression for the point not explicitly made: Jesus, not identified by name in the speech, is the prophet like Moses whom they crucified on the cross.

> Acts 7:40-41 saying to Aaron, 'Make for us gods to go before us; as for this Moses who led us out from the land of Egypt, we do not know what has become of him.' And **they made a calf**[42] in those days, and offered a sacrifice to the idol and rejoiced in the works of their hands.

> Acts 7:40 εἰπόντες τῷ Ἀαρών, Ποίησον ἡμῖν θεοὺς οἳ προπορεύσονται ἡμῶν. ὁ γὰρ Μωϋσῆς οὗτος, ἐξήγαγεν ἡμᾶς ἐκ Αἰγύπτου, οὐκ οἴδαμεν τί ἐγένετο αὐτῷ.

> 7:41 καὶ **ἐμοσχοποίησαν** ἐν ταῖς ἡμέραις ἐκείναις καὶ ἀνήγαγον θυσίαν τῷ εἰδώλῳ καὶ εὐφραίνοντο ἐν τοῖς ἔργοις τῶν χειρῶν αὐτῶν

Ernst Haenchen[43] said that the speech was sacred history with no theme. The theme and focal point of the speech is in verse 7:40 where Luke has Stephen note Aaron's responsibility for the golden calf demonstrating that high priests from the beginning have been wicked tenants. In Luke, The Parable of the Wicked Tenants has been directed against the temple establishment led by the High Priest.[44] Thus, Luke ties together, with this verse, his Gospel with his second book. In doing so, he provides both the theme and the defense to the charges. The Wicked Tenants do not have the jurisdiction to try Jesus, Stephen or Paul.

> 32:4 καὶ ἐδέξατο ἐκ τῶν χειρῶν αὐτῶν καὶ ἔπλασεν αὐτὰ ἐν τῇ γραφίδι καὶ ἐποίησεν αὐτὰ **μόσχον** χωνευτὸν καὶ εἶπεν οὗτοι οἱ θεοί σου Ισραηλ οἵτινες ἀνεβίβασάν σε ἐκ γῆς Αἰγύπτου

---

41. Scroggs, 184.
42. G3447 μοσχοποιέω, to make a calf; alludes to Ex 32:4.
43. Haenchen, Acts, A Commentary, 288.
44. Scribes and chief priests, Lk. 20:19.

Stephen tells us they made an image of a calf which he disparagingly described as an εἰδώλῳ (idol). "The term is used in the LXX for the images and statues of pagan deities, in other words, those deities had no reality and no power since they were the product of fantasy, ..."[45]

The Second Commandment is not so much against images but rather against a mistaken conception of God "in making gods of objects that owe their 'existence' to human hands, people have failed to recognize the true source of existence."[46]

The composer of Nehemiah 9 rewrote scripture changing the maker of the molten calf from Aaron to the people. Stephen used Nehemiah 9 as a model for his last speech and says in agreement, "They made a calf in those days."

The Antiquities of the Jews is a rewriting of sacred history wherein Josephus omitted any mention of the incident of the golden calf and its consequences. This rewriting is directed particularly at Luke because only Luke includes unmistakable references to Enoch, Moses, the golden calf, Elijah, Lot, the Diaspora, covenant-rooted in gathering of the exiles, and a circumcised messiah out of the house of David.

Did Luke identify with the priests and the Northern Levites who are said to have inserted this story of the Golden Calf into Sacred Scriptures as a subtle criticism of the priesthood of the Jerusalem Temple? These priests, who joined the community of the followers of Jesus, liked the Northern Levites, considered the temple establishment in Jerusalem to be idolatrous. In any event Josephus appreciated what Luke has done and thus he rewrote sacred scriptures to eliminate the scriptural support for Acts 7:41 by omitting the golden calf incident from his rewriting of sacred scripture.

"Stephen's entire speech is directed towards pointing out the continuing obduracy of Israel against God. (Cf. Acts 7:25, 35, 39, 40–41, 51–53)."[47]

45. Schnabel, Commentary on Acts, 381.
46. Pearce, "Philo and the Second Commandment, 74.
47. Litwak, Echoes of Scripture in Luke-Acts, 186.

Moses

The unknown author of The Epistle of Barnabas made a radical conclusion based upon his interpretation of the golden calf incident. He suggested that when Moses "cast the two tables from his hands" because the Israelites had turned to idols, they lost the covenant. Ellen Juhl Christiansen has stated: This idea "is actually expressed in the Septuagint text which contains a sentence that is not in the MT. Thus Jeremiah 31:32 LXX reads after 'not the covenant I made with their ancestors, when I took them by the hand to bring them out of Egypt;' then the LXX adds: 'for they did not abide in my covenant and I had no concern for them, says the LORD.' This means the covenant is not just broken, rather it is no longer valid."[48] Thus, Barnabas could have based his radical conclusion on the addition to the LXX text appearing in Jeremiah 31:32. Therefore, the generally accepted view that Barnabas relied upon an anti-Jewish source or tradition needs to be revisited.

"If covenantal identity is seen against the background of other expressions of a collective self-understanding in the Old Testament, there are several important terms that also reflect covenantal belonging. Since they play a role in both intertestamental literature and the New Testament, I shall mention them as possible alternative or replacement categories. Thus, the Hebrew word for "people" (of God) is an inclusive term, used of Israel as a totality with the underlying assumption that belonging to the people of Israel is through birth (footnote omitted)."[49] This Hebrew term is translated over 1500 times in the Septuagint as λαὸν. This Greek word appears numerous times in the New Testament as follows: Matthew, 13 times; Mark, 3; Luke, 37; John, 3; Acts, 47 and in the remainder of the New Testament, 29 times. Someone who writes a book tying his history to the whole course of the salvation history of God's people wherein λαὸν is used 84 times in Luke-Acts and the people are the recipient of God's promised deliverance, is not writing about the rejection of God's people.

Much of what we read in Acts 7:41–50 has appeared in Jeremiah 7. In verses 24–26 the following words appear:

---

48. Christiansen, The Covenant in Judaism, 56.
49. Christiansen, 5–6.

24 But they did not obey or incline their ear, but walked in their own counsels and the stubbornness of their evil hearts, and went backward and not forward. 25 From the day that your fathers came out of the land of Egypt to this day, I have persistently sent all my servants the prophets to them, day after day; 26 yet they did not listen to me, or incline their ear, but stiffened their neck. They did worse than their fathers.

The temple sermon preached by Jeremiah provided Stephen with the inspiration for his speech.

Chapter 7

The Temple

Acts 7:42 But God turned and gave them over to worship the host of heaven,[1] as it is written in the book of the prophets[2]:

'Did you offer to me slain beasts[3] and sacrifices, forty years in the wilderness, O house of Israel?'

With this statement, Israel Knohl contends that the Prophet Amos mocked the cultic practice and sacrificial worship in the Sinai desert.[4] It would be more accurate to state that Amos, who was the boldest of the prophets, concluded there should be no animal sacrificial system. Thus, Stephen, in agreement with Amos, unlike the Lucan Jesus, condemned the animal sacrificial system.

Acts 7:43 And you took up the tent of Moloch, and the star of the god Rephan, the figures which you made to worship; and I will remove[5] you beyond[6] Babylon.'

1. The "host of heaven" is found in the LXX in Neh 9:6. et al.
2. Alludes to Jer. 7:18 and Jer. 19.13.
3. G4968 σφάγιον is a rare word, hapax in the NT, Acts 7:42.
4. Knohl, The Sanctuary of Silence, 215.
5. G3351 μετοικίζω is a rare word in the NT; Acts 7:4, 43.
6. G1900 ἐπέκεινα is a rare word in the NT; Acts 7:43, 44.

In Acts 7:42–43, the concept of *lex talionis* is introduced with the Greek verb, παρέδωκεν, alluding to Wisdom 11:16. Israel's worship of the host of heaven occurs during the period of Assyrian domination in the eighth century B.C.E.[7] Stephen changes the "beyond Damascus" phrase from Amos 5:27 to "beyond Babylon" to make the prophecy refer to Judah not Samaria. The quotation in bold in Acts 7:42–43 is from Amos 5:25–27.

7:42 ἔστρεψεν δὲ ὁ θεὸς καὶ παρέδωκεν αὐτοὺς λατρεύειν τῇ στρατιᾷ τοῦ οὐρανοῦ καθὼς γέγραπται ἐν βίβλῳ τῶν προφητῶν Μὴ σφάγια καὶ θυσίας προσηνέγκατέ μοι ἔτη τεσσαράκοντα ἐν τῇ ἐρήμῳ οἶκος Ἰσραήλ

7:43 καὶ ἀνελάβετε τὴν σκηνὴν τοῦ Μολὸχ καὶ τὸ ἄστρον τοῦ θεοῦ ὑμῶν Ῥεμφάν, τοὺς τύπους οὓς ἐποιήσατε προσκυνεῖν αὐτοῖς καὶ **μετοικιῶ ὑμᾶς ἐπέκεινα** Βαβυλῶνος

Amos 5:25 μὴ **σφάγια καὶ θυσίας προσηνέγκατέ μοι ἐν τῇ ἐρήμῳ τεσσαράκοντα ἔτη οἶκος Ισραηλ**

Amos 5:26 **καὶ ἀνελάβετε τὴν σκηνὴν τοῦ Μολοχ καὶ τὸ ἄστρον τοῦ θεοῦ ὑμῶν** Ραιφαν τοὺς τύπους αὐτῶν οὓς ἐποιήσατε ἑαυτοῖς

Amos 5:27 καὶ **μετοικιῶ ὑμᾶς ἐπέκεινα** Δαμασκοῦ λέγει κύριος ὁ θεὸς ὁ παντοκράτωρ ὄνομα αὐτῷ

Steyn makes several important observations about the use of the Amos quotation and the phrase "beyond Damascus" in Acts 7:42–43.[8] First, the quotation is the turning point in the speech serving as the transition between past cultic practice and present cultic practices.

Secondly, the Amos quotation is interpreted in four different contexts: "The MT reflects a Mesopotamian astral context, the Damascus Scroll which reflects a Jewish sectarian context, the Septuagint (LXX) reflecting a Judean-Hellenistic context and Acts

---

7. Knohl, 218.
8. Steyn, Trajectories of Scripture Transmission, 1–7.

The Temple

7 reflecting an early Christian context."[9] In the second context, the Damascus Scroll has used the Amos quotation "as justification for those who separated themselves from the priesthood in Jerusalem" using "Damascus" as a code word for their sectarian community at Qumran.[10]

Amos 5:25 cited in Acts 7:42 rehearses Israel's forty years of wandering in the wilderness, along with its failure to truly honor God during this time. Idolatry was a pattern of Israel's behavior. Even the creation itself, sun, moon, stars, trees, animals, has become an idol. The heavenly bodies are repeatedly mentioned in Holy Scriptures as representing false deities whom Israel and the nations worshipped.[11] Stephen asserts that Israel worshipped not only the golden calf but also "the host of heaven" (τῇ στρατιᾷ τοῦ οὐρανοῦ), i.e., sun, moon and stars. "Israel's willingness to "turn back" resulted in God turning his back on Israel."[12] Stephen's use of the Amos passage is similar to that found in the Damascus Document, CD VII, 14–17.[13]

The Greek phrase καὶ παρέδωκεν αὐτοὺς (and delivered them up) in Acts 7:42 is also found in Psalm 106:41 (LXX 105) καὶ παρέδωκεν αὐτοὺς εἰς χεῖρας ἐθνῶν καὶ ἐκυρίευσαν αὐτῶν οἱ μισοῦντες αὐτούς.

"The hymnody of Israel likewise connects the great acts of God's redemption in the exodus and contrasting act of their infidelity in the episode."[14] Psalm 106:19–22 states:

> They made a calf in Horeb and worshiped a molten image. They exchanged the glory of God for the image of an ox that eats grass. They forgot God, their Savior, who had done great things in Egypt, wondrous works in the land of Ham, and terrible things by the Red Sea.

---

9. Steyn, n.p.
10. Steyn, n.p.
11. LXX numerous; Amos 5:25–27; Acts 7:41–43.
12. Schnabel, 381.
13. Davilia, editor, The Dead Sea Scrolls as Background, 126.
14. Lints, Identity and Idolatry, 36.

"The retelling of the story of Israel's redemption is contrasted with the story of the making of the idol. God brought Israel out of bondage and gave them life. In turn they made idols and became like their idols, without life."[15] Rejection of God and his activity brings judgment. Israel's idolatry of the golden calf resulted in Israel's exile. Consequently, God allowed the people "to become captive to the consequences of their own evil choices"[16] "that they might learn that one is punished by the very things by which he sins."[17]

"The first principle of worship is to offer it to Yhwh alone; the second is to offer it without the use of images (Ex 20:3-6)."[18] "The second presupposes the near-universal practice of making images as aids in worship."[19]

For other examples of such summaries in the Septuagint, see Deut. 6:20-24; 26:5-10; Josh. 24:2-13; 1 Sam. 12:8-13; Neh. 9:6-31; Ps. 78:5-72; 105:7-44; 106:7-46; 135:5-12; 136:4-25; Ezek. 20:5- 29; Jdt. 5:6-19; 1 Macc. 2:52-60; Wis. 10:1—11:1; Sir. 44:3-50:21; 3 Macc. 2:4-12; 6:4-8; and the following non-Septuagint texts: 1 En. 85:3-90:38; 93:3-10; 91:11-17; 2 Bar. 56:2—74:4; 4 Ezra 3:4-36; 14:2933; Sib. Or. 3:248-94; CD II, 17-IV, 12; Josephus, J.W. 5.379-412; Ant. 3.86-87; 4.40-49. This list was compiled by Benjamin J. Snyder, The "Fathers" Motif in Luke-Acts.[20]

> Acts 7:44 Our fathers had the tent of witness in the wilderness, even as he who spoke to Moses and directed him to make it, according to the pattern that he had seen.
>
> 7:44 Ἡ σκηνὴ τοῦ μαρτυρίου ἦν ἐν τοῖς πατράσιν ἡμῶν ἐν τῇ ἐρήμῳ καθὼς διετάξατο ὁ λαλῶν τῷ Μωσῇ, ποιῆσαι αὐτὴν κατὰ τὸν τύπον ὃν ἑωράκει

---

15. Lints, Identity and Idolatry, 96.
16. Johnson, Acts of The Apostles, 131.
17. Wisdom 11:16 (RSV).
18. Goldingay, Israel's Life, 127.
19. Goldingay, Israel's Life, 127.
20. Journal of Inductive Biblical Studies, 2/2:44-71.

The Temple

"A movable tent was a more suitable shrine for a pilgrim people than a fixed structure like the Jerusalem temple. Stephen's narrative has already illustrated the impossibility of restricting the divine presence to any one locality."[21] This tent of witness stands in contrast to the "tent of Moloch" of the previous verse. It is probable that the Israelites appropriated the heavenly tent of EL from the Canaanites.[22]

Tent of witness Ex 27:21

27:21 ἐν τῇ σκηνῇ τοῦ μαρτυρίου ἔξωθεν τοῦ καταπετάσματος τοῦ ἐπὶ τῆς διαθήκης καύσει αὐτὸ Ααρων καὶ οἱ υἱοὶ αὐτοῦ ἀφ' ἑσπέρας ἕως πρωὶ ἐναντίον κυρίου νόμιμον αἰώνιον εἰς τὰς γενεὰς ὑμῶν παρὰ τῶν υἱῶν Ισραηλ

In Verses 44–50, Stephen mentioned the "tent of witness" and suggested that God does not live in a place "made with hands." The "tent of witness," the sanctuary designed by God, was first located in the wilderness near Mt. Sinai (Ex 27:21). The "tent of witness" was moved (Joshua 18:1) to Shiloh when they took possession of the land. The "tent of witness" was still functioning in 1 Samuel 2:22. David expressed his desire to build a temple (2 Sam. 7:2) because "the ark of God dwells in a tent. Nathan voices God's disapproval saying, "I have not dwelt in a house since the day I brought up the people of Israel to this day, but I have been moving about in a tent for my dwelling" (2 Sam. 7:6). Shiloh is located approximately 44 kilometers north of Jerusalem, in the hills of Ephraim in Samaria.

Moses is receiving the "pattern" for the "tent of witness" at the same time Aaron is making the golden calf. When Stephen tells the story of the golden calf (7:41) in his retelling he says, following Neh. 9:18, "they made a calf," deflecting the blame from Aaron.

Stephen's criticism may really be that the "idol" language is the distortion of the "image of God" which distortion is emphasized by the footstool quotation from Isaiah. This image of idolatry is in stark contrast to the image of the angelic face of Stephen in

---

21. Bruce, 205.
22. Clifford, The Tent of El, 221–27 and fn 3.

Acts 6:15 who "gazed into heaven and saw the glory of God" and the "son of man" (Acts 7:55–56). Stephen is saying, with his earlier quotation from Amos, that the narrative of idolatry runs from the incident of the golden calf to the present day. Since Stephen is following several summaries including Joshua 24 and Nehemiah 9, he could have easily mentioned the gods which your fathers served beyond the River, and in Egypt (Joshua 24:2,14). Joshua, like Stephen, also used the expression, "your fathers." The "tent of witness," like Shechem, is identified as Samaritan.

Stephen also seems to say that the belief, that the Temple is the abode of God, is a form of idolatry. It may be more accurate to say, in agreement with Pao, that criticism is against the people, not the Temple.[23]

> Acts 7:45–50. "there was in fact nothing especially Christian in these views . . . ."[24] It is clear from "intertestamental" literature such as 1 Enoch, Jubilees, Psalms of Solomon and the Dead Sea Scrolls that prominent scribal groups sharply condemned the high priestly rulers.

> Acts 7:45 Our fathers in turn brought it in with Joshua when they dispossessed[25] the nations which God thrust out before our fathers. So, it was until the days of David,

> Acts 7:45 ἦν καὶ εἰσήγαγον, διαδεξάμενοι, οἱ πατέρες ἡμῶν, μετὰ Ἰησοῦ ἐν τῇ κατασχέσει τῶν ἐθνῶν ὧν ἐξῶσεν ὁ Θεὸς ἀπὸ προσώπου τῶν πατέρων ἡμῶν, ἕως τῶν ἡμερῶν Δαυίδ,

There was no need for the tent of Moloch since our ancestors had the tent of meeting in the wilderness which Joshua and the people brought across the river Jordan into the land. This tent was still in the land and functioning at Shiloh[26] in the time of David.

> Acts 7:46 who found favor in the sight of God and asked leave to find a habitation for the God of Jacob.

---

23. Pao, Acts and the Isaianic New Exodus, 207, fn 74.
24. Mendels, The Rise and Fall of Jewish Nationalism, 311–312.
25. G1237 διαδέχομαι LXX several; Acts 7:45.
26. Josh. 18:1; 1 Sam. 2:22.

7:46 ὃς εὗρεν χάριν ἐνώπιον τοῦ θεοῦ καὶ ᾐτήσατο εὑρεῖν σκήνωμα τῷ Θεῷ Ἰακώβ

Although this verse conceptually alludes to Gen 33:8,10, the language clearly forms an allusion to LXX Ps. 131:5, "who found favor in the sight of God and asked leave to find a habitation for the God of Jacob."[27]

> Psa 132:5 until I find a place for the LORD, a dwelling place for the Mighty One of Jacob."

> 132:5 ἕως οὗ εὕρω τόπον τῷ κυρίῳ **σκήνωμα τῷ θεῷ Ιακωβ**

DeWaard instructs us that the speech contrasts the worship of Moloch (τὴν σκηνὴν τοῦ Μολοχ, Amos 5:26) with the tent of witness (Ἡ σκηνὴ τοῦ μαρτυρίου, v.44) and with the dwelling place for the God of Jacob (σκήνωμα τῷ Θεῷ Ἰακώβ, (v.46). The opposite of τοὺς τύπους οὓς ἐποιήσατε (Amos 5:26) is ποιῆσαι αὐτὴν (*i.e.* τὴν σκηνὴν, Amos 5:26) κατὰ τὸν τύπον ὃν ἑωράκει (v.44). ὁ ὕψιστος (the Most High, v.48), to whom the prophetical word is applicable: ὁ οὐρανός μοι θρόνος (heaven is my throne) functions as an opposite to τοῦ θεοῦ ὑμῶν Ραιφαν, (Amos 5:26), to which is alluded in v.42 by λατρεύειν τῇ στρατιᾷ τοῦ οὐρανοῦ.[28]

> Acts 7:47 But it was Solomon who built a house for him.

> Acts 7:47 Σολομῶν δὲ οἰκοδόμησεν ὑτῷ αὐτῷ οἶκον.

> Act 7:48 Yet the Most High does not dwell in houses made with hands; as the prophet says,

The word χειροποιήτοις "(made with human hands) always refers to idols in the Greek Old Testament and is without exception a negative reference in the New Testament."[29] Seven out of the nine appearances of the word χειροποιήτοις in the canonical text of the LXX appear in Isaiah[30], and in all nine passages the term is

---

27. Johnson, 133.
28. DeWaard, Study of the OT Text in the Dead Sea, 46.
29. Beale, We Become What We Worship, 192.
30. Isa 2:18; 10:11; 16:12; 19:1; 21:9; 31:7; 46:6.

used in reference to idols. "The misuse of the temple is therefore considered an act of idolatry."[31]

N.T. Wright has informed us "made by hand" is a recommendation for good quality merchandise which we should purchase.[32] Wright then tells that the prophets have told us in my words it is utter nonsense to worship something you have made with your hands.[33]

> "The prophet Isaiah (66:1–2) clearly stated that God's transcendence cannot be limited to a house and that a distinction must be maintained between the creator whose hand made all these things and houses made with hands. Otherwise, one does not worship God 'in this place' (vv 7, 49–50), but commit idolatry."[34]

> "Judaism never taught that God actually lived in the temple or was confined to its environs but spoke of his 'Name' and presence as being there. In practice, however, this concept was often denied."[35]

> Acts 7:49 'Heaven is my throne, and earth my footstool, What house will you build for me, says the LORD, or what is my place of rest?

> Acts 7:49 Ὁ οὐρανός μοι θρόνος ἡ δὲ γῆ ὑποπόδιον τῶν ποδῶν μου ποῖον οἶκον οἰκοδομήσετέ μοι λέγει κύριος ἢ τίς τόπος τῆς καταπαύσεώς μου

> Isa. 66:1 οὕτως λέγει κύριος ὁ οὐρανός μοι θρόνος ἡ δὲ γῆ ὑποπόδιον τῶν ποδῶν μου ποῖον οἶκον οἰκοδομήσετέ μοι ἢ ποῖος τόπος τῆς καταπαύσεώςμου

"This is the only place where *earth* itself is the divine *footstool*. In 1 Chronicles 28:2 and Psalms 99:5 and 132:7 the house

---

31. Pao, Acts and the Isaianic New Exodus, 207.
32. N.T. Wright, Acts for Everyone, Part One, 116.
33. Wright, 117.
34. Krodel, 151.
35. Longenecker, 142.

The Temple

itself, or the ark within the house, is the footstool, ..."[36] The word "footstool" in verse 49 alludes to Ps. 110.1; 109.1 LXX where the same Greek word is used, ὑποπόδιον. [37]

Moyter states: "There is no justification for writing a post-exilic scenario for a passage like this; it is as pre-exilic as Solomon's temple and as Isaianic 1:10–20."[38]

This is the first indication that Stephen's (and also Luke's) attitude toward the Jewish temple has changed. Luke had a positive view of the temple of Jerusalem up until Acts 7:48, 49, when he highlighted Stephen, who quoted Solomon, saying, "'The Most High does not dwell in houses made by human hands; as the prophet says: "Heaven is My throne, and earth is the footstool of My feet; What kind of house will you build for Me?" says the LORD, 'Or what place is there for My repose?'" Stephen made this statement in the context of his defense before the Sanhedrin (Acts 6:12). He was accused of speaking blasphemous words against "this holy place, and the Law" (v. 13).

The two main passages of Scripture that Stephen quotes are Amos 5:25–27 (in verses 42–43) and Isaiah 66:1–2 (in verses 49–50. Respectively, these deal with the themes of idolatry and God using the world as a footstool – i.e., not contained in a house built by hands.

The Jewish people believed that the Temple was the abode of God. Numerous citations to scripture could be provided but we will rely upon two important passages: Ex 40:34–5 and 1 Kings 8:10–11.

Sometime after coming down the mountain, Moses directed the building of the earthly tabernacle. Once the work was finished, "Then the cloud covered the tent of witness, and the glory of the LORD filled the tabernacle. And Moses was not able to enter the tent of witness, because the cloud abode upon it, and the glory of the LORD filled the tabernacle" (Ex 40:34–5). The same phenomenon is reported of Solomon's temple: "And it came to pass . . .

---

36. Motyer, The Prophecy of Isaiah, 533.
37. G5286; M & M 659; see also Acts 2:35.
38. Motyer, 533.

that the cloud filled the house. And the priests could not stand to minister because of the cloud, because the glory of the LORD filled the house" (1 Kings 8:10–11). But this presence was conditional on the people keeping the covenant faithfully. Only if they do this will God "dwell among the children of Israel, and will not forsake my people Israel" (1 Kings 6:12–13).

When the Temple was rebuilt after the exile, nothing comparable to the Ex 40:34–5 and 1 Kings 8:10–11 experiences occurred yet the people still believed that the Temple was the abode of God. Stephen believed that God had never resided in the Temple, or perhaps, he believed that God had long ago abandoned the Temple. Ezekiel sees the glory of God leave the first Temple (Ezek. 10–11) before the Babylonian destruction. Ezekiel 10:18 and 11:21–23 indicates God's presence left the holy of holies at the beginning of the Babylonian exile and did not return to inhabit the temple constructed after the return from exile.

Stephen "condemned the very existence of the Temple, describing its construction as an act of idolatry."[39] Even the priests defiled Solomon's Temple with the idols of nations.[40]

There is no criticism of David by Stephen for asking that he might find a dwelling place nor of Solomon for building God a temple. Nathan did criticize voicing God's disapproval "I have not dwelt in a house since the day I brought up the people of Israel from Egypt to this day, but I have been moving about in a tent for my dwelling."[41]

The building of the temple by Solomon is described in 1 Kings 5:1–7:51. When the temple is completed, the "tent of meeting" with ark of the covenant is brought into the temple (1 Kings 8:4). The tent is not mentioned again. Solomon in his dedication speech[42] said "But will God indeed dwell on the earth? Behold, heaven and the highest heaven cannot contain thee; how much less this house which I have built!" and expressed the same theology

---

39. Scharlemann, *Stephen*, 7.
40. 2 Chron. 36:14.
41. 2 Sam 7:6.
42. 1 Kings 8:27

as the passage cited in Isaiah. Likewise, Goldingay has noted that "Heaven is like the throne on which YHWH actually sits. The earth is like the footstool on which the divine feet then rests." That fact makes a laughing stock of the notion that people will then build a house where God can relax."[43] In the OT, "the presence of the LORD is not confined to the Temple."[44] Although not stated, Greene resolves the idolatry issue raised by Stephen by indicating the "Spirit" of God is present.

Act 7:48–50 Yet the Most High does not dwell in houses made with hands; as the prophet says, (49) 'Heaven is my throne, and earth my footstool[45]. What house will you build for me, says the LORD, or what is the place of my rest? (50) Did not my hand make all these things?'

The appeal to scripture is a major theme of Luke-Acts and is devastatingly effective with its citation to Isaiah in Acts 7:51–53 when Stephen pointedly matched his audience with their 'fathers' as does Paul when he issues his stern rebuke in Acts 28:25–27 quoting Isaiah 6:9–10. Stephen relies on a quotation from the book of Isaiah which was composed before the construction of the first temple.

> The phrase "most high" occurs in 34 verses in the RSV in the OT without "God" immediately before or after the phrase (but only twice in the Pentateuch, Num 24:16 and Deut 32:8, MT and SP) and only once in Acts but four times in Luke and nowhere else in the NT.
>
> Num 24:16 the oracle of him who hears the words of God, and knows the knowledge of the Most High, who sees the vision of the Almighty, falling down, but having his eyes uncovered:
>
> (oracle of Balaam) SP Num 24:16
> The oracle of him who hears the words of El,
> And knows the minds of Ileeyyone [most high]

43. Goldingay, Isaiah, 370; see also 2 Kings 19:15; Lam 2:1.
44. Greene, The Spirit in the Temple, 717–42, 721.
45. G5286 ὑποπόδιον; LXX, numerous; Acts 7:49.

> Deut 32:8 When the Most High gave to the nations their inheritance, when he separated the sons of men, he fixed the bounds of the peoples according to the number of the sons of God.

> SP Deut 32:8 When Ileeyyone gave the nations their inheritance, when he separated the sons of Aadaam, He set the borders of the peoples according to the number of the sons of Yishraae.

Stephen's reference to the idolatrous golden calf being the result of "the works of their hands" only a few verses earlier (Acts 7:41) makes it clear that Stephen has idolatry in mind in verse 48 when he refers to Israel's temple as "made by hands."

> Acts 7:50 Did not my hand make all these things?'

> Acts 7:50 οὐχὶ ἡ χείρ μου ἐποίησεν ταῦτα πάντα ?

This is a rhetorical question in Acts while in Isaiah LXX it is a statement. Luke uses the question to allude to 7:42. The rhetorical question prepares the way for the condemnation which follows in the conclusion of the speech.

Matthias Klinghardt[46], cited by Seland[47], observed that the speech switches from *argumentatio* in Acts 7:50 to *peroratio* in 7:51. The resulting condemnation led to outrage and the stoning.

Beale noted that "the stone mountain of Daniel[48] was not made with human hands"[49] and that "Christ identified himself[50] with the stone of Daniel, the true Temple."[51]

Bart Koet notes "In Israel history there are two trends: a positive one which is modelled upon the promise to the fathers and a negative one, modelled upon their obduracy."[52]

---

46. Klinghardt, *Gesetz und Volk gottes*, J.C.B. Mohr, 286.
47. Seland, *Hellenists, Hebrews, and Stephen*, 189.
48. *Dan.* 2:34, 45.
49. *Beale,* The Temple and the Church's Mission, 225.
50. Luke 20:18
51. Beale, 226.
52. Koet, Five Studies, 97–118.

CHAPTER 8

End of Speech

Acts 7:51 "You stiff-necked[1] people, uncircumcised[2] in heart and ears, you always resist[3] the Holy Spirit. As your fathers did, so do you.

Acts 7:51 Σκληροτράχηλοι καὶ ἀπερίτμητοι καρδίαις καὶ τοῖς ὠσίν, ὑμεῖς ἀεὶ τῷ

Πνεύματι τῷ Ἁγίῳ ἀντιπίπτετε; ὡς οἱ πατέρες ὑμῶν, καὶ ὑμεῖς.

Roth has provided several examples demonstrating that the first audience would have to be familiar with the LXX. Acts 7:51, "uncircumcised in hearts and ears" is from the LXX: Lev. 26:41; Jer. 6:10; Ezek. 44:4,7.[4] The phrase "circumcision of the heart" also occurs in Deut. 10:16; 30:6; Ezek 44:7-9; 1QpHab 11:13; and Rom 2:29.[5] We should also add "stiff-necked" which is from LXX Duet. 9:6; 31:27.

This statement identifies the Sanhedrin as the enemy of the Holy Spirit. The shift from "our fathers" (Abraham, Isaac, Jacob

1. G4644 σκληροτράχηλος is a hapax in the NT. LXX several.
2. G564 ἀπερίτμητος is a hapax in the NT; LXX several.
3. G496 ἀντιπίπτω is a hapax in the NT; LXX several, Acts 7:51.
4. Roth, Blind, Lame and Poor in Luke-Acts, 86.
5. See Lemke, "Circumcision of the Heart," 299–319.

81

and Moses) to "your fathers" who resisted God's word and appointed leaders established a boundary line between the two communities. The followers of Jesus refused to be identified with those who resist the Holy Spirit.

Stephen turns to overt use of invective when the pronoun is changed to "your" fathers (7:51–52).[6] The reference to fathers "throughout the speech is essential to the reversal achieved in the speech."[7] Thus, the pattern of reversal of fortunes, which is a significant part of the structure of Luke's gospel as proclaimed in the Magnificat is again realized. However, the step progression of reversals within the speech should be noted: 7:4 vs 43; 7:7 vs 42 and 7:8 vs 51.

According to Jervell, "The idea of the Spirit as the distinguishing mark of the people of God permeates the whole of Acts. Stephen is characterized by an irresistible Spirit (6:5,10; 7:55), and it is therefore absurd to accuse him of speaking against Israel, that is against the law, the temple and Moses (6:11,13,14; 7:51–3)."[8]

In this verse, Stephen was acting out the role of a prophetic preacher of penitence to Israel, and almost all that he said was borrowed from sermons or prayers of penitence to Israel in the Old Testament. Compare the following: "But [the desert generation] and our ancestors . . . stiffened their necks and did not obey your commandments. . . . They were disobedient and rebelled against you and cast your law behind their backs and killed your prophets, . . . and they committed great blasphemies (Neh 9:16, 26; read the whole of 9:6–37)."[9]

Why O LORD did you . . . harden our hearts . . . ."[10]

Steck, as noted by Moessner, has demonstrated that "The history of Israel is one long, unending story of a 'stiff-necked and disobedient people.'"[11] More than half of the speech is devoted

---

6. Litwak, "your fathers," also occurs in Lk 11:47–48; 186.
7. Penner, 306.
8. Jervell, The Theology of the Acts of the Apostles, 46.
9. Skarsaune, 26 *In the Shadow of the Temple*, 1.
10. Isaiah 63:17.
11. Moessner, 'The Christ Must Suffer' compiled by Orton, 122.

to Moses and the Exodus.[12] The role of the calf in this retelling is an extremely important event in the history of the resistance of a stiff-necked people.

As noted earlier, Antiochus IV abolished, *inter alia*, the laws pertaining to circumcision. Thus, Hellenism influenced the decision of parents not to circumcise their boys and resulted in many men in Jerusalem being uncircumcised. The fact that Stephen ends his speech with an accusation that his audience is stiff-necked and uncircumcised in heart and ear is not meant to spiritualize circumcision or make trivial the physical rite.

Luke "uses a technique familiar in the OT and post-OT Jewish writings, by putting a theological statement in the form of a speech or song recounting the history of Israel from ancient times (Josh 24:1–18; Psalms 105:12–45; 106:6–46; Judith 5:5–21; 1 Enoch 84–90; Acts 13:16–41): but whereas all these other examples finish with a promise or celebration of God's salvation, this speech builds up to a climax of condemnation."[13]

No other New Testament writing charges the Jews as dramatically with the responsibility of the death of Jesus. After Pentecost, Peter (Acts 3.14–15; 4.27) and then Stephen (Acts 7.51–3) denounce the Jews as the murderers of Jesus. It is in conformity with this unified solidarity against Jesus that Peter and Stephen will remember, without any distinction among the people of Jerusalem, this Jesus 'you have killed' (Acts 3.15; 4.10; 7.52).

The purpose of Acts 7:46–52 is to conclude that "As Moses was rejected and the people's worship became blasphemous thereby [Acts 7:20—43], so with *Christ* rejected, the *Temple worship* becomes a blasphemy."[14]

However, it is important to note that these stiff-necked Jews on two memorable occasions risked their necks. In the Book of Esther, we read: "And Mordecai would not bow down."[15] Mordecai was obstinate; stiff-necked. Josephus relates that during the reign

---

12. Acts 7:17–44.
13. Maddox, The Purpose of Luke-Acts, 52–53.
14. Kilgallen, Stephen Speech, 94.
15. Esther 3:2.

of Caligula, the Roman Emperor had ordered that a statue of him be installed in the Temple precincts. Josephus tells us 10,000 Jews met Petronius in Ptolemais and told him "But if you are wholly resolved to bring the statue and install it, then you must first kill us, and then do what you have resolved. For while we are alive, we cannot permit such things as are forbidden by our law. . . ."[16]

The people were stiff-necked. They were ready to die for their faith. "Just as Jesus fulfills the role of the suffering Mosaic servant"[17] so does his witness Stephen.

> Acts 7:52–53 Which of the prophets did not your fathers persecute? And they killed those who announced beforehand the coming[18] of the Righteous One, whom you have now betrayed and murdered, (53) you who received the law as delivered by angels[19] and did not keep it."
>
> Acts 7:52 τίνα τῶν προφητῶν οὐκ ἐδίωξαν οἱ πατέρες ὑμῶν ; καὶ ἀπέκτειναν τοὺς προκαταγγείλαντας περὶ τῆς ἐλεύσεως τοῦ Δικαίου, οὗ νῦν ὑμεῖς προδόται καὶ φονεῖς ἐγένεσθε,
>
> Acts 7:53 οἵτινες ἐλάβετε τὸν νόμον εἰς διαταγὰς ἀγγέλων, καὶ οὐκ ἐφυλάξατε.

We find this theme of Killing the Prophets in several places in Luke-Acts: Lk 6:22–23; 11:47–51; 13:33–34 and Acts 7:52. In addition, this motive may also be in the background of the Parable of the Wicked Tenants.[20]

The accusation, of killings the prophets, is based on rather slim evidence.[21] The Prophet Uriah is the only named prophet who is killed in Jewish Scripture.[22] Both Acts 7:52 and Nehemiah 9 include the same Greek words for "killed" and "prophets" in the

---

16. Josephus, Ant. 18.8.
17. Beker, *Heirs of Paul*, 55.
18. G1660 ἔλευσις LXX none; Acts 7:52.
19. Angels mediate covenants appears in 4Q470, Gal. 3:19; Heb 2:2.
20. Lk 20:9–19.
21. Amaru, The Killing of the Prophets, Vol. 54, 153–180, 154.
22. Amaru, 154 citing Jer. 26:20–24.

same sentence. It is likely that Luke relied upon Nehemiah 9:26 (RSV) which states:

> Nevertheless, they were disobedient and rebelled against thee and cast the law behind their back and killed thy prophets, who had warned them in order to turn them back to thee, and they worked great blasphemies.

Since Luke used Nehemiah 9 as an outline for his last speech, it is likely this is his source.

> Persecution of the prophets is common in the OT, which, although it notes only one example of such rejection to the point of murder, does echo similar complaints (1 Kings 18:4, 13; 19:10, 14; Jer. 2:30; 26:20–24; 2 Chron. 24:20–21 [Zachariah, son of Jehoiada, the priest, is stoned]; . . . . The Qumran document 4QpHos 2.2–6 says 'they cast behind their backs all his precepts' (LeCornu and Shuman 2003: 267)."[23]

Judaism does not recognize Zachariah, son of Jehoiada, the priest, as one of the 55 recognized prophets. Bock does not recognize that Uriah, the only named prophet who is killed in Jewish Scripture, is a prophet.

Luke's use of the term "the Righteous One" in Acts 3:13–15; 7:51–53 and 22:14–15 is probably based upon 1 Enoch 38 since in all of these passages "the Righteous One" is the eschatological agent of God. The designation in Acts appears only in speeches delivered to Jewish audiences in Jerusalem. VanderKam has noted "that the single [prior] case in which 'Righteous One' is used as an individual title of the eschatological leader is 1 En 53:6."[24] The title of 'righteous one' may have its provenance in Isa 53:11.

According to Moses in his final speech (LXX Deut 33:2) said "at his right, angels with him."

Stephen's speech is atypical in that most of the twenty characteristics that Kurz concluded are characteristics of great classic

---

23. Bock, *Baker Commentary*, 305.
24. VanderKam, The Righteous One in 1 Enoch 37–71", 170–171.

farewell speeches and the four of biblical speeches were not present with one notable exception: a theological review of history.[25]

Acts 7:51-53 "Stephen clearly charged that his hearers stand in continuity with the worst elements of Israel past. And they themselves are more reprobate than their fathers for their fathers murdered the prophets, whereas they themselves have now betrayed and murdered the Righteous One."[26]

---

25. Kurz, Luke 22:14-38 and Farewell Addresses, 251-268, 262.
26. Cassidy, Society and Politics in the Acts, 35.

CHAPTER 9

Reaction

Acts 7:54 Now when they heard these things, they were **enraged**[1], and they ground[2] their teeth against him.

7:54 Ἀκούοντες δὲ ταῦτα **διεπρίοντο** ταῖς καρδίαις αὐτῶν καὶ ἔβρυχον τοὺς ὀδόντας ἐπ' αὐτόν

C OMPARE

Acts 5:33 Οἱ δὲ ἀκούσαντες **διεπρίοντο** καὶ ἐβουλεύοντο ἀνελεῖν αὐτούς

They were furious.

Acts 7:55–56 But he, full of the Holy Spirit, gazed into heaven and saw the glory of God, and Jesus standing at the right hand of God; (56) and he said, "Behold, I see the heavens opened, and the Son of man standing at the right hand of God."

Acts 7:55 ὑπάρχων δὲ πλήρης Πνεύματος Ἁγίου, ἀτενίσας εἰς τὸν οὐρανὸν, εἶδεν δόξαν Θεοῦ καὶ Ἰησοῦν ἑστῶτα ἐκ δεξιῶν τοῦ Θεοῦ,

---

1. G1282 διαπρίω is double hapax; LXX 1 Chron 20:3.
2. G1031 βρύχω LXX numerous, hapax in Acts 7:54.

Acts 7:56 καὶ εἶπεν, Ἰδοὺ, θεωρῶ τοὺς οὐρανοὺς διηνοιγμένους, καὶ τὸν Υἱὸν τοῦ ἀνθρώπου ἐκ δεξιῶν ἑστῶτα τοῦ Θεοῦ.

Both Jesus and Stephen are "filled with the holy spirit," (πλήρης Πνεύματος Ἁγίου; Luke 4:1; Acts 7:55).

"Only here does the title **Son of man** occur outside the Gospels and on the lips of someone other than Jesus"[3] recalling that Jesus at his trial responded to a question about his identity as the Christ by saying, "from now on the Son of man shall be seated at the right hand of the power of God" (Luke 22:69).

Acts 7:57 But they cried out with a loud voice and stopped[4] their ears and rushed together upon him.

7:57 κράξαντες δὲ φωνῇ μεγάλῃ **συνέσχον τὰ ὦτα αὐτῶν** καὶ ὥρμησαν ὁμοθυμαδὸν5 ἐπ' αὐτόν συνέσχον τὰ ὦτα αὐτῶν

The people believed they heard blasphemy, Lev. 24:14; Num 15:35 and responded with mob violence. They stopped their ears is a subtle allusion to Isaiah 6:10 where the LORD said, "stop their ears."

Jer 6:10 To whom shall I speak and give warning, that they may hear? Behold, their ears are closed, they cannot listen; behold, the word of the LORD is to them an object of scorn, they take no pleasure in it.

Jer 6:10 πρὸς τίνα λαλήσω καὶ διαμαρτύρωμαι καὶ ἀκούσεται ἰδοὺ ἀπερίτμητα **τὰ ὦτα αὐτῶν** καὶ οὐ δύνανται ἀκούειν ἰδοὺ τὸ ῥῆμα κυρίου ἐγένετο αὐτοῖς εἰς ὀνειδισμόν οὐ μὴ βουληθῶσιν αὐτὸ ἀκοῦσαι

Zec 7:11 But they refused to hearken, and turned a stubborn shoulder, and stopped their ears that they might not hear

---

3. Krodel, 155.
4. G4912 συνέσχον, BDAG, 971; M & M 606–7.
5. G3661 ὁμοθυμαδὸν with one accord; M & M 448.

7:11 καὶ ἠπείθησαν τοῦ προσέχειν καὶ ἔδωκαν νῶτον παραφρονοῦντα καὶ **τὰ ὦτα αὐτῶν** ἐβάρυναν τοῦ μὴ εἰσακούειν

Jer 5:21 "Hear this, O foolish and senseless people, who have eyes, but see not, who have ears, but hear not.

Jer 25:4 You have neither listened nor inclined your ears to hear, although the LORD persistently sent to you all his servants the prophets,

25:4 καὶ ἀπέστελλον πρὸς ὑμᾶς τοὺς δούλους μου τοὺς προφήτας ὄρθρου ἀποστέλλων καὶ οὐκ εἰσηκούσατε καὶ οὐ προσέσχετε τοῖς ὠσὶν ὑμῶν

Acts 7:58 Then they cast him out of the city and stoned him; and the witnesses laid down their garments at the feet of a young man named Saul.

Acts 7:58 Καὶ ἐκβαλόντες ἔξω τῆς πόλεως, ἐλιθοβόλουν. καὶ οἱ μάρτυρες ἀπέθεντο τὰ ἱμάτια αὐτῶν παρὰ τοὺς πόδας νεανίου καλουμένου Σαύλου.

Krodel suggests that Luke did not understand the judicial procedure set forth in Lev. 24:10-14 for death by stoning.[6]

Deuteronomy 17:2-7 states that stoning was to take place outside the city gates, and that the witnesses to the criminal act were to be the first to stone the convicted criminal. Leviticus 24:24 makes the same point: "Bring forth him that has cursed outside the camp; and let all that heard him lay their hands upon his head, and let all the congregation stone him."

Acts 7:59 And as they were stoning Stephen, he prayed, "LORD Jesus, receive my spirit."

Acts 7:59 Καὶ ἐλιθοβόλουν τὸν Στέφανον, ἐπικαλούμενον καὶ λέγοντα, Κύριε Ἰησοῦ, δέξαι τὸ πνεῦμά μου.

The correspondence to Jesus' last word is clear. Stephen's witness is climaxed by echoing Jesus' dying breath, "LORD Jesus,

---

6. Krodel, 153; Deut 17:2-7.

receive my spirit" (Acts 7:59=Luke 23:46; cf. Acts 7:52 with Luke 23:47).

> Acts 7:60 And he knelt down and cried with a loud voice, "LORD, do not hold this sin against them." And when he had said this, he fell asleep.
>
> Acts 7:60 θεὶς δὲ τὰ γόνατα, ἔκραξεν φωνῇ μεγάλῃ, Κύριε, mē μὴ στήσῃς αὐτοῖς αὐτὴν τὴν ἁμαρτίαν. καὶ τοῦτο εἰπών, ἐκοιμήθη.

Jesus' first word from the cross corresponds to Stephen's last word.

It has been frequently noted that Stephen's call for forgiveness echoes Jesus' plea from the Cross in Luke 22:34. It also alludes to the stoning of Zacharias and his plea for vengeance.

Chapter 10

The Enigma of Acts 8:1

And Saul was consenting[1] to his death[2]. And on that day a great persecution arose against the church in Jerusalem; and they were all scattered[3] throughout the region of Judea and Sama'ria, except the apostles.

Acts 8:1 Σαῦλος δὲ ἦν συνευδοκῶν τῇ ἀναιρέσει αὐτοῦ. Ἐγένετο δὲ ἐν ἐκείνῃ τῇ ἡμέρᾳ διωγμὸς μέγας ἐπὶ τὴν ἐκκλησίαν τὴν ἐν Ἱεροσολύμοις. πάντες δὲ διεσπάρησαν κατὰ τὰς χώρας τῆς Ἰουδαίας καὶ Σαμαρείας, πλὴν τῶν ἀποστόλων.

Stephen in his speech portrayed a history of idolatry and unfaithfulness to God. His charge has OT precedent (Neh. 9:17; Ezek. 20:8, 123) and the language is like Exod. 16:3 and Num. 14:3-4. Schneider believed the persecution was directed against the Hellenists. He erroneously believed that Stephen represented the Hellenists.[4]

---

1. G4909 συνευδοκέω, 1 & 2 Macc. per BDAG, 970; Acts 8:1.
2. G336 ἀναίρεσις LXX several; 2 Macc. 5:13; Acts 8:1; 22:20.
3. G1289 διασπείρω, LXX numerous; Acts 8:1, 4; 11:19.
4. Bock, *Baker Commentary*, 318 citing G. Schneider, *Die Apostelgeschichite*, vol. 1, (1980), 479.

About the year 200 BCE, there arose among the Jewish population a group called Hellenists, who adopted Greek culture as a way of life to such a degree that, almost invariably, they gave up their Jewish culture and identity. The Hellenizers "sought the complete dissolution of the characteristics of Judaism and its consistent assimilation to its Hellenistic environment."[5] "According 2 Maccabees 4:13, these events marked 'an extreme of Hellenization' (ἀκμή τις Ἑλληνισμοῦ) in Jerusalem."[6] The book of Jubilees was also extremely critical of the Hellenizers and their goals.

The Maccabees won. As Hengel noted, "a severe 'collective trauma' remained, despite the victory, and this had a decisive influence on the further course of Jewish history."[7] The reaction of Palestinian Judaism to Hellenism led to "extreme sensitivity of Palestinian Judaism towards even an apparent usurpation of power over the law and the sanctuary."[8] This explains the severe reaction against Stephen. The small Jewish group of the followers of Jesus "could only maintain itself in Palestine by strict observance of Torah."[9]

Samaritans as "keepers of the law" strongly disliked the Hellenizers as did the Judeans. Only the Hellenists were persecuted. This conclusion is supported by the fact " . . . that the reason for (and not the result of) the banishment was the mission of the Hellenists among Diaspora Jews and above all among non-Jews. Perhaps this is the real background of Stephen's martyrdom."[10]

In reading the various Jewish texts written during the Hellenistic reforms and the Maccabean wars, it is apparent that the authors were concerned with the issue of mixed marriages (exogamy). In fact, mixed marriages are rejected. Lange notes that "The Book of the Words of Noah in 1QapGen ar, the Book of Watchers, the Aramaic Levi Document, the Temple Scroll, and the Book of

   5. Hengel, *Judaism and Hellenism*, 305.
   6. Hengel, *Judaism and Hellenism*, 75.
   7. Hengel, *Judaism and Hellenism*, 305.
   8. Hengel, *Judaism and Hellenism*, 306.
   9. Hengel, *Judaism and Hellenism*, 309.
   10. Stegemann, *The Jesus Movement*, 219–220.

Tobit points towards a rejection of intermarriage by the majority of Judean Jewry in early Hellenistic times."[11] Earlier biblical texts had prepared the way with criticism of mixed marriages.[12]

We read about intermarriage during the Hellenistic religious reforms as evidenced by 1 Macc. 1:11–15.

> 11 In those days lawless men came forth from Israel, and misled many, saying, "Let us go and make a covenant with the Gentiles round about us, for since we separated from them many evils have come upon us." 12 This proposal pleased them, 13 and some of the people eagerly went to the king. He authorized them to observe the ordinances of the Gentiles. 14 So they built a gymnasium in Jerusalem, according to Gentile custom, 15 and removed the marks of circumcision, and abandoned the holy covenant. They joined with the Gentiles and sold themselves to do evil.

"Not only did they build a gymnasium and removed their circumcision, thus abandoning the holy covenant, they also joined the nations sexually by intermarriage."[13] The Book of Jubilees uses the story of Dinah from Genesis 34 as a warning against intermarriage with the nations. Jubilees puts the language from Deut. 7:3 into the words spoken by the angel to show all intermarriages are forbidden. Its rationale is that intermarriage defiles the family and the whole of Israel as a holy seed and its sanctuary as well. (Jub. 30:8, 13–15). "For Jubilees, intermarriage endangers the cultic and religious integrity and identity of Judaism."[14] There was nothing more radical in the Jewish writings than the call of Judaism for separation from the nations.[15] Mixed marriages threaten the identity of the community. "Frevel and Conczorowki theorize that exogamy seems to have been a burning issue during early Hellenistic times. The community had to redefine their identity under

---

11. Lange, "Significance of Pre-Maccabean Literature", 183.
12. Num 12:1; 1 Kings 11:1–13; 16:31–33.
13. Lange, "Mixed Marriages" edited by Frevel, 208.
14. Lange, "Mixed Marriages" edited by Frevel, 218.
15. Frevel, "Separate Yourself in Mixed Marriages", 220.

new circumstances."[16] In like manner, the Hellenists of Acts 6 and 7 threaten the identity of the community of the followers of Jesus.

Schmithals notes that, from the early days, there was a "party", or faction, in the Jerusalem church that observed the law and another that did not. The Hellenists, those who did not observe the law, were persecuted by the Jews and fled Jerusalem, while those who observed the law were unmolested: "Therefore, for the Jewish Christian in Palestine in the question of their attitude to the law was not only, perhaps not even principally, a theological problem, but a question of their existence as a Church in the Jewish land."[17]

The Hellenists were chased out of Jerusalem because they threatened the religious identity and integrity of the nascent Jewish Christianity. They chased the Hellenists out to comply with their understanding of Ezra 6:19–21 and Neh. 10–29–30 and its command to separate themselves from the impurity of the people of the land. The irony of the persecutions of Acts 8:1 is that it demonstrates the exclusivity of Judaism, specifically Jewish Christianity as practiced by the Hebrews and Judeans followers of Jesus in Jerusalem and the inclusivity of Hellenistic Christianity.

> Acts 8:1 "And on that day a great persecution arose against the church in Jerusalem; and they were all scattered[18] throughout the region of Judea and Sama'ria, except the apostles."

As noted, only the Hellenists were persecuted. The Hebrews were not persecuted. Thus, the enigma. The Hebrews as Samaritans were outcasts who had been excluded from the Temple. The Samaritans disliked the Hellenists. In the Introduction, five groups were identified:

1. members of the Sanhedrin;
2. the group that includes the Apostles and those worshipping in the Temple every day;

---

16. Venter, Pieter M., "The dissolving of marriages", n.p.
17. Schmithals, *Paul and James*, SBT 1/46 (London, SCM, 1965), 39.
18. G1289 διασπείρω, LXX numerous; Acts 8:1, 4; 11:19.

3. the Hellenists;
4. members of the synagogue that disputed with Stephen;
5. and the Hebrews.

Thus, the Hellenists were chased out by members of the Sanhedrin and the group that included the Apostles and the Hebrews. However, that is the enigma that cannot be resolved. In the Excursus, Criticism of the Apostles, three strange incidents were identified to which a fourth must be added: did the Apostles, all of whom have been named saints, participate in the persecution against the Hellenists?

Dyer, in a footnote, has astutely suggested that the inclusion of Samaritan Christians in Acts 6–7 "may have led to the first 'confessional schism' of the early church."[19] Even though Luke states that "a great persecution arose against the church in Jerusalem; and they were all scattered," it seems to be the consensus of scholars that the persecution exclusively targeted the "hellenists" on the grounds that Stephen is a "hellenist" and that the Apostles remained in Jerusalem. In the next verse, using hidden polemics, Luke reveals Stephen is a Samaritan.

---

19. Keith Dyer, "*Conflicting Contexts in Prophecy*", 206, fn 31.

Chapter 11

Burial

Acts 8:2 Devout[1] men buried[2] Stephen, and made great lamentation[3] over him.

8:2 συνεκόμισαν δὲ τὸν Στέφανον ἄνδρες εὐλαβεῖς καὶ ἐποίησαντὸ **κοπετὸν μέγαν** ἐπ' αὐτῷ

Gen 50:10 When they came to the threshing floor of Atad, which is beyond the Jordan, they lamented there with a very great and sorrowful lamentation; and he made a mourning for his father seven days.

50:10 καὶ παρεγένοντο ἐφ' ἅλωνα Αταδ ὅ ἐστιν πέραν τοῦ Ιορδάνου καὶ ἐκόψαντο αὐτὸν **κοπετὸν μέγαν** καὶ ἰσχυρὸν σφόδρα καὶ ἐποίησεν τὸ πένθος τῷ πατρὶ αὐτοῦ ἑπτὰ ἡμέρας

Initially we note that the Greek word εὐλαβεῖς for devout and the Greek word κοπετὸ for lamentation are both Lucan rare words appearing only in Luke-Acts. It may be that verse 2:5 which states, "Now there were dwelling in Jerusalem Jews, devout men

---

1. G2126 εὐλαβής LXX Lev. 15:31; Micah 7:2; Sir 11:17; Lk 2:25; Acts 2:5; 8:2; 22:12.
2. G4792 συγκομίζω; Job 5:26; Acts 8:2
3. G2870 κοπετός Gen 50:10; Zech 12:10,11; various; Acts 8:2.

BURIAL

from every nation under heaven" and verse 8:2 form an *inclusio* with "devout men" as the bookends. These Jews had respect for Stephen and his views and saw him as a noble and righteous man, a man like Simeon.

This Greek word εὐλαβεῖς appears in the Septuagint in two places of interest with two different meanings.[4] In Lev. 15:31, the LXX states: "You shall make the sons of Israel be cautious εὐλαβεῖς because of their uncleanness." Secondly in Micah 7:2, the LXX reading says: "For the devout εὐλαβής ones are destroyed and there does not exist one keeping straight among men." ST, MT and LXX of Lev 15:31 all have the "sons of Israel."[5]

Luke suggests that Stephen was such a devout man that devout men buried and made lamentation over him. Yet other men considered Stephen to be so unclean that they stoned him. They stoned him because he was a Samaritan which Luke discloses with his rare word allusion to Lev 15:31 because the phrase "sons of Israel" denotes the Samaritans. Stephen was a Samaritan "waiting on tables" continuing the table-fellowship ministry to the new outcasts, Greek speaking Jews who had forsaken Jewish ways and to Hebrew speaking Samaritans. These people were excluded from the Temple because they were not considered Jewish. This is the real background of Stephen's martyrdom.

The Greek phrase κοπετὸν μέγαν only appears in Acts 8:2 and Genesis LXX 50:10 which is part of the narrative of Joseph burying his father in the land of Canaan beyond the Jordan at the cave that Abraham had purchased as a burial site. Today Hebron is known as the city of the Patriarchs because it is believed to be the location of the cave site purchased by Abraham. In fact, this hapax alerts the audience that a place location shift had occurred in Stephen's Sermon, suggesting that this is a type of hidden polemics.

There are four separate mentions in Genesis of the purchase of this burial site that Abraham had purchased (Genesis 23; 25:9–10; 49:29–32; 50:13). Joseph made his brothers promise that he will be buried at this site where Jacob his father had been buried.

---

4. Muraola, *Greek-English Lexicon of the Septuagint*, 301.
5. The RSV has translated this phrase as "people of Israel."

However, when the people of the Exodus transported his casket to its final resting place, the bones of Joseph were buried at Shechem in the burial site that Jacob had purchased (Joshua 24:32). Stephen in his last sermon stated: "and Jacob went down into Egypt. And he died, himself and our fathers, and they were carried back to Shechem and laid in the tomb that Abraham had bought for a sum of silver from the sons of Hamor in Shechem."

Luke, in alluding to Genesis 50:10 in Acts 8:2, with his use of the Greek phrase, κοπετὸν μέγαν, is telling us he is aware of the two burial site traditions and that Stephen had used a burial tradition offensive to the temple establishment. At the same time Luke is disclosing that Stephen has employed hidden polemics in his speech in his use of the place name, Shechem, associated with the Samaritans.

This Greek phrase κοπετὸν μέγαν for "great lamentation" also appears in 1 Maccabees 2:70; 4:39; 9:20 and 13:26. The death of Mattathias is described in these words: "And he died in the hundred forty and sixth year, and his sons buried him in the sepulchres of his fathers at Modin, and all Israel made great lamentation for him." The third and fourth citations describe the death and burial at Modin of Judas and Jonathan respectively. 1 Macc. 4:39 describes how the men mourned with great lamentation when "they saw the sanctuary [at Mount Zion] desolate, the altar profaned, and the gates burned."

Luke intends to direct our attention to the conflict and opposition between Hellenism and Judaism that arose in the time of the Maccabees and more particularly to his identification of the Hellenists (perhaps more accurately Hellenizers) of Acts 6 with the Hellenizers of 1 Maccabees, a group strongly disliked by the Samaritans.

"In those days there emerged in Israel lawless men who persuaded many, saying, 'Let us go and make a covenant with the nations that are around us; for since we separated ourselves from them, many evils have come upon us'" (I Maccabees 1:11 RSV). In 1 Maccabees, the Hellenizers are described as "godless," "lawless," "lawbreakers," and "men who hate their own nation." The

BURIAL

Hellenizers are criticized in 1 and 2 Maccabees but not by this name; Jubilees, 1 Enoch, Daniel and Sirach are also highly critical. None of these texts use a Greek word which can be translated as Hellenizers.

We started commenting that Luke in the Greek phrase translated as "great lamentation" was alluding to the Maccabees. Recall that Acts 8:2 states: "Devout men buried Stephen, and made great lamentation over him." Perhaps Luke is asking the First Reader to recognize that in the Maccabean period, thousands of devout men were called upon to die or lose their traditional way of life. Stephen was stoned for continuing the table fellowship ministry of Jesus. They said Jesus ate with sinners, but Stephen ate with a large group of sinners and by his actions threaten the boundaries of Judaism and the political structure of the temple establishment.

The 'Hellenizers' in Maccabees and in the first century include many priests and high-ranking members of the temple establishment. Just as "the author of 1 Maccabees refrains from accusing the leading Hellenizers of idolatry"[6], so does Luke. This is surprising considering the strong anti-idol polemic that appears throughout Acts of the Apostles. It may however explain why many priests joined the movement. They were conservative, more so, than the ranking members of the temple establishment.

Stephen's last sermon is really a dialogue with more than one group. Stephen successfully challenged the Hellenizers and they complained to the temple establishment. Both the Hellenizers and the temple establishment were happy to eliminate Stephen. Saul originally challenged the Hellenizers, but he like the temple establishment also had opposed Stephen, because Stephen wanted to include within Judaism those members on the fringe. Stephen and the Samaritans were both adamantly opposed to the Hellenizers because the Hellenizers wanted to remove those parts of Jewish practice that separated Jews from others: dietary laws, Sabbath observance, and circumcision. It was an unusual dialogue!

With the Greek phrase, κοπετὸν μέγαν, for "great lamentation", Luke alludes to the death and burial of Jacob in Genesis 50:10

---

6. Goldstein, *1 Maccabees*, 199.

LXX and of Mattathias in 1 Maccabees 2:70 and perhaps also to their last speeches.

Mattathias said to his sons:

> Now, my children, show zeal for the law, and give your lives for the covenant of our fathers. Remember the deeds of the fathers, which they did in their generations; and receive great honor and an everlasting name. Was not Abraham found faithful when tested, and it was reckoned to him as righteousness? Joseph in the time of his distress kept the commandment, and became lord of Egypt. Phinehas our father, because he was deeply zealous, received the covenant of everlasting priesthood. Joshua, because he fulfilled the command, became a judge in Israel. Caleb, because he testified in the assembly, received an inheritance in the land. David, because he was merciful, inherited the throne of the kingdom forever. Elijah because of great zeal for the law was taken up into heaven. Hannaniah, Azariah, and Mishael believed and were saved from the flame. Daniel because of his innocence was delivered from the mouth of the lions. And so, observe, from generation to generation, that none who put their trust in him will lack strength. (1 Macc. 2:50–61).

Perhaps Stephen recognizing he was about to die composed his speech inspired in part by the last speech of Mattathias. Certainly, Mattathias has set forth some inspirational examples. Earlier, Stephen had stated that that Abraham lived in the land "yet he [God] gave him no inheritance in it" using the Greek word κληρονομία for inheritance. Mattathias specifically notes that Caleb received an inheritance κληρονομίαν in the land. Joshua and Caleb were the only spies who reported favorably. They were the only ones of the all the people who left Egypt who were permitted to enter the promised land. Caleb was the leader of the Israelites after Joshua and is buried with Joshua in Samaria. Caleb is not mentioned by name by Stephen because his inheritance was Hebron and the region around it which was in Judea.

BURIAL

Stephen's use of the Righteous One as a term for Jesus may have been influenced by the last speech of Mattathias. Although Paul developed his argument about righteousness of Abraham from Genesis 15:6, the statement in Mattathias's last speech, and Jubilees 23:10, does demonstrate that first century Judaism considered Abraham to be a model of obedience to God. Unlike Mattathias and Paul, Stephen makes no mention of the righteousness of Abraham.

This rare word allusion that Luke makes in Acts 8:2 to Leviticus 15:31 is the strongest clue that Stephen and the Hebrews are Samaritans. Initially this rare word allusion is a hidden polemic that is particularly devastating for several reasons. Luke uses step progression method by introducing the Samaritans in Luke 9:51–55 (the people would not receive Jesus); Luke 10:37 (the one who showed mercy on him) and Luke 17:16–18 (He was a Samaritan). Luke also uses step progression with the phrase "sons of Israel" in Luke 1:16; Acts 7:23 and 37. As Krodel stated, "Luke never says everything at once, but expands and unfolds earlier themes as he moves step by step from one episode to another."[7]

The theory of the rationale of Luke in presenting information as he did in Luke 16 and Acts 6–7 is already recognized but to my knowledge the theory has not been applied to the writings of Luke. According to Yairah Amit, "A polemic is said to be hidden when its subject is not stated explicitly or when it is not stated in the usual or expected manner or wording."[8] The phenomenon of polemics is found throughout the whole corpus of biblical literature. Amit includes the "Northern Population" which would later be known as the Samaritans, as one of the subject matters of hidden polemics. It may be that the hidden polemic of Waiting on Tables is intermarriage with Samaritans.

Yairah Amit argues that several biblical texts displaying "hidden polemics" can be read as a reflection of inner-Judean conflicts. In her view, the authors chose this genre because they may not have been in a position to address these polemics in the open. It

---

7. Krodel, *Acts*, 281
8. Amit, *Polemics*, 138.

is also possible that one or more of the authors may have been practicing irenical theology.

The book of "Leviticus was the heart and soul of the priestly community at Qumran"[9] and Lev 15:31 is "the key to understanding the community's emphasis on purity."[10] With this allusion, Luke is reminding his audience that we need fewer self-centered legalists and more appreciative and more caring merciful Samaritans.

Furthermore, Luke's allusion to Micah 7:2 LXX is a devastating attack on the Sanhedrin, the court that tried Stephen. The *Hermeneia Commentary on Micah* with respect to verse 7:2 states: The reverent εὐλαβεῖς one "is in this context, one who practices the expected pieties toward fellow man and God. All such are gone and the greed and injustice have gone so far that one would have to fear to practice traditional virtues. It is the courts that are the worst, to judge from the difficult text (cf. Micah 3:1–4, 9–12)."[11]

Finally, in first century, the Samaritans called themselves "the sons of Israel" while the Jews referred to themselves as the Judeans. In many instances the phrase "sons of Israel" is recognized as all-inclusive referring to both Judeans and Samaritans. However, in this polemic context, as in 2 Kings 17:7–8; Jer. 32:30, 32; 2 Ch. 13:12 and Amos 3:1, it is a reference to the Samaritans.

Thus, the audience had been prepared by step progression for the allusion to υἱοὺς Ἰσραήλ, ("the sons of Israel") in Leviticus. Step progression with the respect to "the sons of Israel" began with an extremely subtle allusion in verse 6:1 in the use of the rare word γογγυσμός directing attention to the murmuring alluded to in Exodus 16:7, 8, 9, 12. Verses 9–10 state:

> And Moses said to Aaron, "Say to the whole congregation of the sons of Israel, 'Come near before the LORD, for He has heard your murmurings.'" And as Aaron spoke to the whole congregation of the sons of Israel,

---

9. Metso, *Evidence from the Dead Sea Scolls*, 76, fn17.
10. VanderKam and Flint, *Meaning of the Dead Sea Scrolls*, 176.
11. Hillers, *Micah*, 85.

they looked toward the wilderness, and behold, the glory of the LORD appeared in the cloud.

The next step in the progression occurs in Stephen's speech in 7:23, 37 which both include υἱοὺς Ἰσραήλ, ("the sons of Israel"). In Amos 3:1 MT, the prophet initiates his covenant lawsuit with these words: "Hear this word that the LORD has spoken against you, O sons of Israel, against the whole family which I brought up out of the land of Egypt." The prophetic message of Amos is "essentially indictments of Israel for breach of covenant."[12]

God sent Amos, a Judean prophet, to warn the northern kingdom of their impending doom. Stephen saw himself as a prophet like Amos but, in this instance, he is one of the Sons of Israel warning the Judeans.

We can make this remarkable claim because Rashi, 12th century Jewish theologian, in discussing Lev. 15:31 MT ("Thus you shall keep the sons of Israel separate from their uncleanness by defiling my tabernacle which is in their midst,") in his Commentary stated:

> And you shall separate Heb. The term always denotes separation (Torath Kohanim 15:196); similarly, "they drew backwards" (Isa. 1:4); and similarly, "the one separated from his brothers" (Gen. 49:26).

Genesis 49:26 states: The blessings of your father are mighty beyond the blessings of the eternal mountains, the , the bounties of the everlasting hills; may they be on the head of Joseph, and on the brow of him who was separate from his brothers. The Samaritans claim Jacob as their father and trace their ancestors to Ephraim and Manasseh, the sons of Joseph, "the one separated from his brothers."

In like manner, in the rare word allusion to Lev. 15:31, MT and LXX, Luke is disclosing that Stephen is one of "the sons of Israel" and a Samaritan, a member of one of the target audiences specified in the commission to the Apostles and to Paul as set forth in Acts 9:15.

---

12. Mendenhall, *Law and Covenant in Israel*, 72.

Gale has indicated that "The reader is particularly likely to detect allusion where the language is in some way 'marked' . . . for example through the use of *hapax legomena* or other uncharacteristic vocabulary."[13] This finding is further confirmed by Leonard's third principle: "Shared language that is rare or distinctive suggests a stronger connection than does language that is widely used."[14] In this instance, we have two shared phrases. Leonard's fourth principle states: "Shared phrases suggest a stronger connection than do individual shared terms."[15]

In the discussion of Acts 6:1, the statement was made "that the evidence is not missing; it has been hidden." The allusion in Acts 8:2 to Lev 15:31 and Micah 7:2 disclosed the missing evidence and now permits us to state the implication. It is surprising that Stephen alluded to Amos, who was a Judean prophet sent to warn the northern kingdom. But it would be more accurate to state that it is ironic that Stephen, one of the sons of Israel and a Samaritan is now warning the southern kingdom.

It should not be surprising that Stephen, a Samaritan, alluded to Amos. S. Lowry said:

> "No Samaritan would or could say, 'which of the prophets have not your ancestors persecuted?' [Acts 7:52] All the later prophets are regarded by the Samaritans as imposters; for this very reason alone, it would be ridiculous to put extra-Pentateuchal quotations into the mouth of a Samaritan."[16] More recently Ingrid Hjelm said "It would be hard to argue for a Samaritan context in the use of Old Testament prophets or the defense of those prophets who had 'announced beforehand the coming of the Righteous one'. The quotations from Amos and Isaiah, the most hated prophets in Samaritan tradition, seem unthinkable in this contest."[17]

---

13. . Gale, *Vergil on the Nature of Things: The Georgics*, 6.
14. . Leonard, "Identifying Inner-Biblical allusions", 251.
15. . Leonard, "Identifying Inner-Biblical allusions", 252.
16. *Principles of Samaritan Bible Exegesis*, (Brill, 1977) 56.
17. The Samaritans and Early Judaism, 119.

BURIAL

My very good Jewish friend and law partner for twenty-five years regularly quoted scripture and was not averse to quoting the New Testament. Being able to quote your opponents' scripture is a good rhetorical technique to employ. It provides the basis for a devastating attack. An appeal to authority is more effective if the assertion of authority is to one accepted by your opponent because you do not have to establish the source as authoritative. Scripture is accepted as authoritative because it is the word of God.

Acts 7:43 quotes Amos 5:26 LXX "you brought along the tent of Moloch" which suggests that during the wilderness years the Israelites worshiped Moloch and continued to do so until the time of the Prophet Amos and beyond. Since Molock is a member of the "host of heaven", verse 43 explains the reference to the "host of heaven" in the preceding verse. The worship of the "host of heaven" which included the sun, moon, stars and planets, was one of the earliest forms of idolatrous veneration (Deut. 4:19, 17:3; 2 Kings 17:16, 21:3, 5; 23:4; Jer. 8:2, 19:13; Zeph. 1:5). The Book of Deuteronomy twice specially distinguishes the host of heaven as objects which the Israelites should not worship. Jeremiah and Zephaniah both record that the cult of the host of heaven had spread from the courts of the Temple to the house-tops in Jerusalem. Luke is the only NT writer to mention the host of heaven.

Quoting Amos 5:25–27, Stephen records God rhetorically asking if Israel had really been offering their sacrifices to Him. Clearly Israel had not. On this basis, Stephen could in effect say, "Don't accuse me of blaspheming the law; check your own history." He could imply this only because he was not a Judean! At the end of the Amos passage, Stephen changed the quote from "Damascus" to "Babylon" to broaden the focus of divine judgment to include the exile of Judah. In the NT, Babylon is a code word for Rome. This unexpected reminder of Judah's disastrous history must have jolted his audience.

Both Judaism and Samaritanism accepted absolute monotheism and the related concern for the avoidance of images. "Even as the Samaritans are shown by anthropology to be the Hebrews of the Hebrews, so a study of their religion and manners demonstrates them to be nothing else than a Jewish sect."[18] According to Coggins, "The Samaritans were even stricter than the Jews in this matter and regarded the Jerusalem cult with suspicion on these grounds."[19] The quotation in Stephen's Sermon from the Prophet Amos was in fact an attack on the emperor worship and iconography in the Jerusalem Temple of the Late Second Temple period. Joseph Gutmann demonstrated that the Judaism of the Hellenistic Roman period was not as aniconic as claimed. He convincingly stated that that "a rigidly and uniformly anti-iconic attitude on the part of the Jews remains as much a myth as the Procrustean bed on which Jewish art history has so often been made to lie."[20]

Although a more detailed study is warranted, it is for our purpose sufficient to note that the war with Rome began in 66 CE when the captain of the temple, Eleazar, son of Ananias, persuaded the temple priests to terminate the twice daily sacrifice for the Roman emperor.[21] This daily offering for the emperor had begun when Judea became a Roman province in 6 CE during the reign of Augustus. The twice daily offerings, described in Num. 28:1–8, are mandated to be provided by the people to be consumed by YHWH.

Since Roman cultic practice made the emperor a god, admitted to the Pantheon and thus became a member of the host of heaven, this daily offering was a form of idolatrous veneration. The Samaritans probably found this divine emperor worship objectionable as well other cultic practices as did the temple priests when Eleazar persuaded them to act. The Prophet Ezekiel accused Israel of bringing idols of other nations into the Temple. Stephen may have done the same when he quoted "the host of heaven" phrase from the Prophet Amos.

Stephen has directed his anti-idol polemics not only against the ancestors of the Judeans but also against all those who worship idols. Those people who worship idols, whether in the Temple

18. Montgomery, *Samaritans*, 27.
19. Coggins, *Samaritans and Jews* citing Montgomery, 91, fn22.
20. Gutmann, J., "Second Commandment", 3.
21. Josephus, *Bellum* 2.409.

or on the housetops, oppose the followers of Jesus. This proposal would be mere speculation but for the fact Luke in Acts 12:20–23 has criticized the ruler cult and its false claim claim of deity with his description of the death of Herod Agrippa.

Chapter 12

Was Stephen a Samaritan?

SCHARLEMANN stated: "It is quite inconceivable that Luke would not have mentioned it."[1] Luke does tell us that Stephen is a Samaritan but to understand how he told us we need to first discuss Luke's use of hidden polemics.

As noted earlier, Luke does not explicitly tell us the ethnic identity of Stephen. "The use of the technique of hidden polemics reflects the existence of different levels of concealment. In those cases, in which the level of concealment is reasonably sophisticated, a good number of readers are likely to fail to recognize the existence of the polemic; . . . ."[2] According to Amit, "those who dwell in Samaria", were the subject of hidden polemics.[3] Yet the Chronicler considered them to be "an integral part of the people of Israel."[4] Notwithstanding the view of the Chronicler, Luke recognized that explicitly disclosing the ethnic identity of Stephen was problematic.

---

1. Scharlemann, *Stephen*, 19.
2. Amit, *Hidden Polemics*, 221.
3. Amit, *Hidden Polemics*, 189–217.
4. Amit, *Hidden Polemics*, 217.

It is generally believed that "the mission among non-Jews begins with Philip outside Jerusalem."[5] This statement presumes that the people being served food in Jerusalem by the community are all Jewish. Perhaps the mission in Jerusalem did not evangelize the poor people who had been excluded from the temple. Therefore, διακονίᾳ is "distribution" not "ministry." As noted earlier, there is no mention of prayer and teaching among those being served food (see comments to Acts 6:4). What "seems unthinkable" is often the most effective rhetorical tool. I call it "thinking outside the box."

---

5. Stegemann, *Jesus Movement*, 219.

Chapter 13

Conclusion

Acts 8:3 But Saul was trying to destroy[1] the church; entering one house after another, he dragged off both men and women and put them in prison.

8:3 Σαῦλος δὲ ἐλυμαίνετο τὴν ἐκκλησίαν κατὰ τοὺς οἴκους εἰσπορευόμενος σύρων τε ἄνδρας καὶ γυναῖκας παρεδίδου εἰς φυλακήν

Acts 8:4 Now those who were scattered went about preaching the word.

8:4 Οἱ μὲν οὖν διασπαρέντες διῆλθον εὐαγγελιζόμενοι τὸν λόγον

Acts 8:5 Philip went down to a city of Sama'ria[2], and proclaimed to them the Christ.

8:5 Φίλιππος δὲ κατελθὼν εἰς πόλιν τῆς Σαμαρείας ἐκήρυσσεν αὐτοῖς τὸν Χριστόν

Luke presents the outreach as beginning first with the Samaritans and then to Hellenistic Jews. Jervell argued that "there ought to be no doubt that Luke regards the Samaritans as

1. G3075 λυμαίνω Ex 23:8; various; Acts 8:3.
2. G4540 Σαμάρεια 11 occurrences in NT but only in Luke-Acts and John.

CONCLUSION

Jews."[3] What the commentators have not recognized is that both groups were served meals by the community in Jerusalem.

It is somewhat of an enigma. However, if you look at the story as one about an emerging religious movement in transition it makes a little bit more sense. In fact, the leaders had to play catch up with zealots spreading the message outside of the circle, as directed by the Risen LORD, apparently before the leaders were ready.

Having completed our exegesis and review of Acts 6 and 7, we can state that the purpose of Stephen's speech is to demonstrate the rebelliousness of the ruling authorities, the devastating effectiveness made possible in part by the Stephen being a Samaritan. It is necessary to recognize that among people marginalized the idea of a substitute is not uncommon and it is not unreasonable to conclude that the community waiting on tables, that was excluded from the Temple, considered their "community as a temple." Stephen was a member of this marginalized community. It is not surprising that a member of a marginalized community, became an activist.[4] For Stephen, the Temple is the heart of the conflict. This conflict begins when an accusation is made that Stephen speaks against the temple (Acts 6:13–14). The violent mob, enraged by his words against the Temple, starts stoning Stephen immediately after he announces that he sees "the Son of Man standing at the right hand of God" (Acts 7:56–58).

When reformers introduce new ideas, they are often met with resistance. Stephen went after the Lost Sheep, the people who had strayed from Judaism. These people were the Samaritans and the Jews who had adopted Greek ways.

What was the reaction of the Temple establishment? Usually, we are told that Stephen became the first martyr and no further analysis is made of the ideas that Stephen may have introduced and the reactions to them. There is no reported reaction to the mission to the Samaritans. It seems that was there was no problem with the Samaritans.

3. Jervell, *Luke and the People of God*, 123.
4. Brettschneider, *Democratic Theorizing from the Margins*, 124.

The Reformation split the Roman Church; it also resulted in the first definitive published statement on Catholic identity when the Council of Trent commissioned the Roman Catechism. Leo XIII declared in 1879 that Aquinas gave the definitive statement of Catholic doctrine but this, of course, was long after the Reformation.

In 37 CE, when Stephen was stoned, there was no definitive statement on Jewish identity. However late in the first century there developed a consensus in Judaism, *inter alia*, rejecting the Septuagint. This probably resulted in the preservation of the Hebrew language at least for religious use and a clear distinction between the Jewish and Christian communities. This was a clear rejection by Jews of Jews who had adopted Greek ways.

CHAPTER 14

Excursus

Criticism of the Apostles

"THE gospel's condemnation of divisiveness among men is one of the most characteristic and appealing elements."[1] Yet Luke does not to appear to weigh in on the matter involving the Hellenists and the Hebrews. Perhaps we have overlooked the criticism of the Apostles because all of them have been named saints.

I seriously doubt that anyone has ever written anything about this topic which I started by reviewing what I initially called a strange incident. Now that I have accumulated three, I saw in my notes that Spencer[2] has criticized the mistreatment of the widows by the Apostles by their neglect due to their devotion to preaching and praying. It is time to recognize what these strange incidents mean to our assessment of the events of Chapter Six and Seven.

The LORD watches over foreigners and sustains the fatherless and the widows[3] but the ministry of meals has fallen short.

1. Niebuhr, *Social Sources of Denominationalism*, 6–7.
2. Spencer, "Neglected Widows in Acts 6:1–7", 715–733..
3. See Psalm 146:9.

What Spencer says about the widows of the Hellenists:

> It is plausible that these Hellenist widows have been cut off from kinship networks in the diaspora and must now depend on local "Hebrew" (Aramaic speaking) residents for basic economic, practical, and social support. Unfortunately, however, these local systems failed to function adequately for the widows in the critical matter of providing food.[4]

Three Strange Incidents

One

In the Greek text of Acts 1:26, Luke is perhaps saying that the election was not divinely sanctioned. He says of the election of Matthias that he was "voted down along with the eleven." The base verb συγκαταψηφίζω [5] means to "vote down "i.e., defeat or, more, to condemn."[6] Since this translation seems inconsistent with the author's attitude toward the Twelve, Stephen C. Carlson says we should inquire whether there are any other passages in Acts which implies the condemnation of the Twelve.

Two

The second strange incident is demonstrated by the juxtaposition of two passages. In the Gospel of Luke, Jesus advocates what has been called servant leadership. One who wants to be leader must first be willing to serve. "For which is the greater, one who sits at table, or one who serves? Is it not the one who sits at table? But I am among you as one who serves."[7] In Acts, we read that the Apostles "summoned the body of the disciples and said, 'It is not

---

4. Spencer, 728
5. G4785 συγκαταψηφίζω; LXX none; Acts 1:26.
6. Thayer's Greek Lexicon
7. Lk 22:27.

EXCURSUS

right that we should give up preaching the word of God to serve tables."[8] In the story of appointment of the deacons, the author has placed the Apostles in a bad light.

Bock states "those who solve the problem come from within the group whose need is greatest."[9] Bock also states: "Since the problems involves Hellenists, Hellenists are given responsibility to solve it."[10] Although Bock makes these statements, Luke has not told us that the Seven are Hellenists, although "The names clearly mark the leaders of the 'Hellenists' as being Greek, . . ."[11] nor has he provided any explicit clues that Stephen is a Hellenist or a Hebrew. "The majority of scholars, however, do consider Stephen to have been a Hellenists, whatever that designation may imply."[12]

Three: Playing Catchup: Blame it on the Samaritans

The reading from Acts 8:14–17 is somewhat of an enigma if you have been attempting to explain why it was necessary for the church in Jerusalem to send Peter and John to Samaria. However, if you look at the story as one about an emerging religious movement in transition it makes a little bit more sense. In fact, the leaders had to play catch up with zealots spreading the message outside of Jerusalem as directed by the Risen LORD apparently before the leaders were ready.

The Apostles had to go to Samaria to validate the mission of Philip because they had initially opposed the mission.

The Hellenists and Hebrews had been excluded from the Temple. Consequently, the Hellenists and the Hebrews were cut off from the Jewish charities[13] and had to set up their own system of poor relief. The Apostles appointed the Seven to wait on tables

---

8. Acts 6:2.
9. Bock, 257.
10. Bock, 261,
11. Penner, 71, fn28.
12. Hill, *Hellenists and Hebrews*, 46.
13. Jeremias discussed the Jewish system of poor relief in *Jerusalem in the Time of Jesus*, 131.

because they considered the Hebrews and Hellenists to be outcasts. There is no mention of Judean members of the followers of Jesus because they had not yet been excluded from the Temple.

It confirms that there was a bit of tension within the movement when the Hellenists murmured against the Hebrews because the widows were being neglected. The tensions existed in part because the Samaritans were doing the neglecting. It is worth noting that Luke considers this dispute to be within the movement and considers the Samaritans to be Jewish.[14]

While we are speculating, perhaps we should consider this a third strange incident as another example where the author is criticizing the Apostles.

Thus, the author in three separate appointment stories has criticized the Apostles. The criticism is rather subtle but perhaps the author was resentful that he was not been selected. Or is it possible that the author has used the person who was not selected as a source for these three stories? Is it possible that the source is the unknown disciple depicted in the pericope, "On the Road to Emmaus"?

Whatever the reason for the criticism, it is likely that the criticism is a type of hidden polemics directed against the leadership because they have handled the food distribution contrary to the teachings of the Lucan Jesus. The teachings of the Lucan Jesus are exemplified, *inter alia*, by the stories involving Samaritans.[15] The polemical discourse is being conducted with unidentified adversaries.

---

14. Acts 11:19 "speaking the word to none except Jews" see also Acts 9:15 RSV

15. Lk 9:52–56; 10:30–37; and 17:11–19.

Bibliography

Amaru, Betsy Halpern. "Killing of Prophets: Unraveling A Midrash." *Hebrew Union College Annual* 54 (1983) 153–80.
Amit, Yairah. "Epoch and Genre: Sixth Century and Growth of Hidden Polemics." In *Judah and Judeans in Neo-Babylonian Period*, edited by Oded Lipschits and Joseph Blenkinsopp, 135–52. Winona Lake, IN: Eisenbrauns, 2003.
———. *Hidden Polemics in Biblical Narrative*. Translated from Hebrew by Jonathan Chipman. Leiden: Brill Academic, 2000.
Baldwin, James. "Creative Process," in *Creative America*, Ridge, NY, NY 1962.
Banks, Robert J. *Paul's Idea of Community*. Rev. ed. Hendrickson, Peabody Mass. 1994.
Barclay, William. *Gospel of Luke*. Rev. ed. Philadelphia PA: Westminster 1975.
Baron, Salo Wittmayer. *Social and Religious History of Jews*, 2nd ed., rev. and enl., Vol. 1, New York: Columbia University 1993.
Barrett. Charles K. *International Critical Commentary (ICC) on Acts of Apostles*, Edinburgh: T. & T. Clark 1994.
Beale, G. K. *We Become What We Worship: Biblical Theology of Idolatry*, Intervarsity, 2008.
_____, *Temple and the Church's Mission*, Intervarsity. 2004.
Beker, Johan Christiaan. *Heirs of Paul*, Fortress, Minneapolis, 1991.
Bloomberg, Craig. "Jesus, Sinners and Table Fellowship" 35-62, *Bulletin for Biblical Research* 19.1 (2009).
Bock, Darrell L. *Baker Exegetical Commentary on New Testament*, Grand Rapids, MI, 2007.
Boin, Douglas. "Hellenistic 'Judaism' and Social Origins of 'Pagan-Christian' Debate", Journal of Early Christian Studies 22 (2014) 167-96.
Bowman. John, translator and editor. *Samaritan Documents Relating to Their History, Religion and Life*, Pickwick Publications, Eugene OR, 1997.
Boyle, Marjorie O'Rourke. "Covenant Lawsuit of Prophet Amos": III 1 - IV 13, *Vetus Testamentum*, Vol. 21, Fasc. 3 (Jul. 1971), pp. 338-362.
Brawley, Robert L. *Luke-Acts and Jews*, SBL, Scholars, Atlanta GA, 1987.

BIBLIOGRAPHY

Brettschneider, Marla. *Democratic Theorizing from the Margins*, Temple University, 2002.

Brodie, Thomas L. "Accusing and Stoning of Naboth (1 Kgs 21:8-13) as Component of Stephen Text (Acts 6:9-14, Acts 7:58a)." *Catholic Biblical Quarterly* 45, no. 3 (July 1, 1983): 426.

Bruce, Frederick Fyvie. *Acts of Apostles: Greek Text with Introduction and Commentary*, third revised and enlarged edition, Grand Rapids: Eerdmanns, 1990.

Cadbury, Henry J. *Making of Luke-Acts*, 2nd ed., Hendrickson, Inc., 1958.

———. Style and Literary Method of Luke, Wipf and Stock, 2001.

Cassidy, Richard J. *Society and Politics in Acts of Apostles*, Orbis Books, Mary Knoll, NY, 1987.

Charlesworth, James H., ed. *Jesus and Archaeology*, Wm B. Eerdman, Grand Rapids MI 2006.

Charry, Ellen T. Brazos, *Psalms 1-50*, Grand Rapids, MI, 2015.

Chouraqui, André. *People and Faith of Bible*, University of Massachusetts, 1975.

Christiansen, Ellen Juhl. *Covenant in Judaism and Paul: Study of Ritual Boundaries as Identity Markers*, Leiden: E.J. Brill, 1995.

Clifford, Richard J. "Tent of El and Israelite Tent of Meeting," Catholic Biblical Quarterly 33 (1971), 221-27.

Coggins, Richard J. *Samaritans and Jews: Origins of Samaritanism Reconsidered*, Atlanta: John Knox, 1975.

Colpe, Carsten. "Oldest Jewish-Christian Community", 90-102, in Christian Beginnings edited by Jurgen Becker, Westminster/John Knox, Louisville, KY, 1987.

Crown, Alan. *Samaritans* (Tubingen: J.C.B. Mohr, 1989).

Dahl, Nils. *Jesus in the Memory of Early Church*, Augsburg Pub. Co., Minneapolis MN, 1976.

Danker, Frederick William, ed. *A Greek-English Lexicon of the New Testament and Other Early Christian Literature*, 3rd Edition, revised, University of Chicago, Chicago IL. 2000.

Davies, William D. *Jewish and Pauline Studies*, Fortress, Philadelphia, 1984.

Davilia, Stephen, ed. *Dead Sea Scrolls as Background to Postbiblical Judaism*, Studies on the Texts of the Desert of Judah, Brill Leiden 2002.

DeWaard, Jan. *Comparative Study of the Old Testament Text in Dead Sea Scrolls and in New Testament*, E.J. Brill, Leiden, 1965.

Dillon, Richard J., *From Eye-Witness to Ministers of the Word*, Rome, Biblical Institute, 1978.

Douglas, Mary. *Purity and Danger*, Routledge, United Kingdom, 1966.

Dunn, James D. G., *Beginning from Jerusalem: Christianity in the Making*, Eerdmans, Grand Rapids, MI 2009.

Dyer, Keith, "Conflicting Contexts in Prophecy and Passion," 190-208, *Essays in Honour of Athol Gill*, edited by David Neville, Australian Theological Forum, Adelaide, Australia 2002

BIBLIOGRAPHY

Endres, John C., *Biblical Interpretation in the Book of Jubilees*, Washington, D.C.: Catholic Biblical Association of America, 1987.

Esler, Philip. *Community and Gospel*, Cambridge University Cambridge 1987.

———. *Conflict and Identity in Romans: The social setting of Paul's letter*, Minneapolis, MN: Fortress, 2003.

Feldman, Louis H. "Rearrangement of Pentateuchal Material in Josephus' Antiquities, Books 1-4" in chapter 14, 309-325 of *Judaism and Hellenism Reconsidered*, Hebrew College Annual 70-71.

Finger, Reta Halteman. *Widows and Meals*, Eerdmans, Grand Rapids, MI 2007.

Fishbane, Michael, *Biblical Interpretation in Ancient Israel* (Clarendon Paperbacks, 1988).

Fitzmyer, Joseph A. *Dead Sea Scrolls and Christian Origins*, Eerdmans, Grand Rapids, MI 2000.

———. *Semitic Background of the New Testament*, Eerdmans, Grand Rapids, MI 1997.

Fletcher-Louis, Crispin. *Luke-Acts: Angels, Christology and Soteriology*, Mohr Siebeck, Tubingen 1997.

Flusser, David. *Judaism of the Second Temple Period*, Vol. 2, Eerdmans, Grand Rapids, MI 2009.

Franklin, Norma. "Samaria from Bedrock to the Omride", *Levant* 36: 189-202. (2004),

Frevel, Christian. "Separate Yourself from the Gentiles" in *Mixed Marriages and Group Identity in the Second Temple Period*, Bloomsbury, USA, 2012.

Goldstein, Jonathan A. *1 Maccabees: a new translation, with introduction and commentary* Garden City, N.Y.: Doubleday, 1976.

Green, Joel. *Theology of the Gospel of Luke*, Cambridge University, Cambridge 1995.

Greene, Joseph R. "The Spirit in the Temple: Bridging the Gap between the Old Testament Absence and New Testament Assumption", *JETS* 55/4 (2012), 717-742.

Gale, Monica R. *Vergil on the Nature of Things: The Georgics, Luretius and the Didactic Tradition*, Cambridge University, 2 Cambridge 2000.

Gaster, Moses. *The Samaritans: Their History, Doctrines and Literature*, Oxford University, London (1925).

Gaston, Lloyd. *No Stone on Another: Studies in the Significance of the Fall of Jerusalem in the Synoptic Gospels*, Supplements to *Novum Testamentum*), Leiden, Brill 1970).

Goldingay, John. *Old Testament Theology: Israel's Life*, InterVarsity, (2003).

Goldstein, Jonathan A. *1 Maccabees: a new translation, with introduction and commentary* (Garden City, N.Y.: Doubleday), 1976.

Guttmann, Joseph, Second Commandment and Image in Judaism, *Hebrew National College*, 32, 1951, 161-174.

Haenchen, Ernest. *Acts of the Apostles: A Commentary*, Westminster, Phila., 1971.

BIBLIOGRAPHY

Halpern-Amaru, Betsy. *The Empowerment of Women in the Book of Jubilees*, SJSJ 60, Leiden: Brill, 1999.

Hayes, Christine. *Gentile Impurities and Jewish Identities: Intermarriage and Conversion from the Bible to the Talmud*, Oxford University (2002).

Helm, Ingrid. *Samaritans and Early Judaism: A Literary Analysis*, JSOT supp. 303, Sheffield, 2000.

Hemer, Colin J. *Book of Acts in the Setting of Hellenistic History*, Tubingen: Mohr, 1989.

Hengel, M. *Judaism and Hellenism*, Wipf and Stock, Eugene OR, 2003.

Kealy, Sean P. *Interpretation pf the Gospel of Luke in the Twentieth Century*, Volume II, Mellen, Lewiston, Me. 2005.

Keener, Craig S. Acts Exegetical Commentary, Baker Academic, Grand Rapids, MI 2013.

Knohl, Israel. *Sanctuary of Silence: Priestly Torah and the Holiness School*, Minneapolis: Fortress, 1995.

Koet, Bart. *Five Studies on the Interpretation of Scripture in Luke-Acts*, SNTA 12 (Leuven: Leuven University, 1989.

Kurz, William. "Luke 22:14-38 and Graeco-Roman and Biblical Farewell Addresses", 104 *JBL* 1985.

Hill, Craig C. *Hellenists and Hebrews: Reappraising Division within the earliest church*, Minneapolis: Fortress, 1991.

Japhet, Sara. *Ideology of the Book of Chronicles and Its Place in Biblical Thought*, Winona Lake, Ind.: Eisenbrauns, 2009.

Jeremias, Joachim. *Jerusalem in the Time of Jesus*, Fortress, Philadelphia, 1969.

Jervell, Jacob. *Luke and the People of God: A New Look at Luke-Ac*ts, Minneapolis 1972.

———. *Theology of the Acts of the Apostles*, Cambridge University, 1996).

Johnson, Luke Timothy. *Acts of the Apostles*, Liturgical, Collegeville, MN 1992

Kilgallen, John. *Stephen Speech*, Biblical Institute, Rome 1976.

Kistemaker, Simon J. *New Testament Commentary: Exposition on the Acts of the Apostles*, Baker, Grand Rapids, MI, 1990.

Klinghardt, Matthias, *Gesetz und Volk gottes*, J.C.B. Mohr, Tubingen, 1988.

Kottsieper, Ingo. "And they did not care to speak Yehudit", 95-124, in *Judah and the Judeans in the Fourth Century B.C.E.*, Eisenbrauns, 2007.

Krodel, Gerhard. *Acts*, (Minneapolis, Minn.: Augsburg, 1986).

Kurz, William. "Luke 22:14-38 and Graeco-Roman and Biblical Farewell Addresses", 104 *Journal of Biblical Literature* (1985), 251-268.

Lange, Armin. "Mixed Marriages and Hellenistic Reforms" in *Mixed Marriages and Group Identity in the Second Temple Period*, edited by Christian Frevel, Bloomburg, USA, 2012.

Lange, Armin. "Significance Of Pre-Maccabean Literature From Qumran Library For the Understanding of Hebrew Bible" in *Congress Volume Ljubljana*, Brill Leiden 2007.

Leonard, Jeffery M. "Identifying inner-Biblical allusions: Psalm 78 as a test case," Journal of Biblical Literature 127, no. 2 (2008), 251.

Bibliography

Lemke, Werner E. "Circumcision of the Heart: Journey of a Biblical Metaphor," in *God So Near: Essays on Old Testament Theology in Honor of Patrick D. Miller*, ed. Brent A. Strawn and Nancy R. Bowen, 299–319. Eisenbrauns, Winona Lake, Ind. 2003.

Levine, Lee. *Judaism & Hellenism in Antiquity*, University of Washington, Seattle, 1998.

Lim, Timothy H. *Holy Scriptures in the Qumran Commentaries and Pauline Letters*, Clarendon, Oxford 1997.

Lints, Richard. *Identity and Idolatry*, InterVarsity, Downers Grove IL, 2015.

Litwak, Kenneth D. *Echoes of Scripture in Luke-Acts: Telling the History of God's People Intertextually*, T&T International, NY 2005.

Longenecker, Richard N. *Expositor's Bible Commentary, Acts*, Zondervan, Grand Rapids, MI, 1995.

Löhing, Karl. "Circle of Stephen and its mission", *Christian Beginnings*, Jürgen Becker, editor, Westminster John Knox, 1993

Lowy, L. *Principles of Samaritan Bible Exegesis*, Brill, 1977.

MacDonald, John. Theology of the Samaritans, The Westminster, Philadelphia, (1964)

MacDonald, Nathan. Priestly Rule: Polemical and Biblical Interpretation in Ezekiel 44, DeGruyter, Berlin Germany, 201).

Maddox, Robert. *Purpose of Luke-Acts*, T. & T. Clark, Edinburgh, 1982.

Magen, Yitzhak. "Dating of the First Phase of the Samaritan Temple on Mt Gerizim in Light of Archaeological Evidence," 157–212, in Oded Lipschitz, Gary N. Knoppers, Rainer Albertz (eds.) *Judah and the Judeans in the Fourth Century B.C.E.*, Eisenbrauns, 2007.

Mare, W. Harold. Acts 7: Jewish or Samaritan in Character?, *Westminster Theological Journal* 34.1 (Nov 1971).

Magness, Jodi. *Stone and Dug, Oil and Spit*, Eerdmans, Grand Rapids, MI, 2011.

Marshall, Howard. *The Gospel of Luke, Commentary on the Greek Text*, Eerdmans, Grand Rapids, MI, 1978.

Mendels, Doron. *Rise and Fall of Jewish Nationalism*, Eerdmans Grand Rapids, MI, 1978.

Mendenhall, George E. *Law and Covenant in Israel and the Ancient Near East* Pittsburgh: Presbyterian Board, 1955.

Metso, Sarianna. "Evidence from the Dead Sea Scolls", in *Editing the Bible: Assessing the Task Past and Present* by John S. Kloppenborg and Judith H. Newman, SBL, Atlanta GA 2012

Metzger, Bruce M. *Textual Commentary on the Greek New Testament*, New York, United Bible Society 2005.

Moessner, David P. "'Christ Must Suffer': New Light on the Jesus – Peter, Stephen, Paul Parallels in Luke-Acts" in *Composition of Luke's Gospel* compiled by David E. Orton, Brill, Leiden, 1999.

Montgomery, James A. *Samaritans, the earliest Jewish sect: their history, theology and literature*, Philadelphia, J.C. Winston, 1907.

Motyer. *Prophecy of Isaiah*, Intervarsity, Downers Grove, Il 1993.

BIBLIOGRAPHY

Moulton, James H. and Milligan, George. *Vocabulary of the Greek New Testament*, Hendrickson, Peabody Mass., 1997.

Munck, J. *Acts of the Apostles*, AB Garden City, NY, 1967.

Muraola, T. *Greek-English Lexicon of the Septuagint*, Peeters, Walpole, MA 2009.

Nelson, Richard D. *Raising Up A Faithful Priest*, Louisville, KY: Westminster/John Knox, 1993.

Newman, Judith. *Praying by the Book, The Scripturalization of Prayer in Second Temple Judaism*, Atlanta: Scholars, 1999.

Niebuhr, Helmut Richard, *Social Sources of Denominationalism*. New York Holt 1957.

Orton, David E. *Synoptic Problem and Q: Selected Studies from Novum Testamentum*, 1999.

Pao, David W. *Acts and the Isaianic New Exodus*, Mohr Siebeck, Tubingen 2000.

———. Waiters or Preachers: Acts 6:1-7 and the Lukan Table Fellowship Motif, Journal of Biblical Literature 130 (2011), 127-144.

Pearce, Sarah. "Philo and the Second Commandment, in Image and its Prohibition, editor, *Journal of Jewish Studies*, Vol. 2 (2013).

Penner, Todd. *In Praise of Christian Origins*, T & T Clark International, New York, 2004.

Petersen, Brian. "Stephen's Speech as a Modified Prophetic Rib Formula", JETS 57/2 (2014), 351-69.

Richard, Earl. *Acts 6:1-8:4: Author's Method of Composition*, Society of Biblical Literature. Missoula, Mont.: Scholars, 1978.

Samkutty, V. T. *The Samaritan Mission in Acts*. New York: T. & T. Clark, 2006.

Sarna, Nahum M. *JPS Torah Commentary on Exodus*, Phila., 1991.

Scharlemann, Martin H. *Stephen: A Singular Saint*, Rome: Pontifical Biblical Institute, 1968.

Schiffman, Lawrence H. *Reclaiming the Dead Sea Scrolls*, Jewish Publication Society 1994.

Schmithals, Walter. *Theology of the First Christians*, Westminster John Knox, Louisville, Kentucky, 1997.

———. *Paul and James*. SBT 1/46 London, SCM, 1965.

Schnabel, Edward J. *Zondervon Exegetical Commentary on Acts*, 2012.

Schorch, Stefan. "Pre-eminence of the Hebrew Language and the Emerging Concept of the 'Ideal Text' in Late Second Temple Judaism" in *Studies in the Book of Ben Sira*, Brill, Leiden, 2008.

———. "Samaritan Version of Deuteronomy and the Origin of Deuteronomy", 23-37 in *Samaria, Samarians, Samaritans: Studies on Bible, History and Linguistics*, edited by Jozsef Zsengeller, De Gruyter, Boston 2011.

———. "What Kind of Authority, Authority of Torah during the Hellenistic and Roman Periods" in *Scriptural Authority in Early Judaism and Ancient Christianity*, de Gruyter, Boston 2013.

Schlatter, Adolf. *Theology of the Apostles*, Baker Books, Grand Rapids MI, 1922.

Scroggs Robin. "Earliest Hellenistic Community" 176-206 in *Studies in the History of Religion* 1968.

BIBLIOGRAPHY

Seland, Torrey. "Once More – Hellenists, Hebrews, and Stephen: Conflicts and Conflict-Management in Acts 6-7," *Recruitment, Conquest, and Conflict*, Scholars, Atlanta 1998.

Sevenster, J. N. *Do you know Greek?*, Brill, Leiden 2014.

Shulam, Joseph, with Hilary Le Cornu, *Commentary on the Jewish Roots of Acts*, Netivyah Bible Instruction Ministry, Jerusalem Israel, 2012.

Siker, Jeffrey S. *Disinheriting the Jews: Abraham in Early Christian Controversy* Westminster/John Knox, Louisville, KY, 1991.

Skarsaune, Oskar. *In the Shadow of the Temple*, InterVarsity, Downers Grove, IL 2002.

Soards, Marion L. *Speeches in Acts: their content, context, and concerns*, Louisville, KY: Westminister/John Knox, 1994.

Spencer, Franklin Scott, "Neglected Widows in Acts 6:1-7," CBQ 56, 715-733, 1994.

Stambaugh, John E., and David L. Balch. *New Testament in Its Social Environment.* Philadelphia: Westminster Press, 1986

Stefon, Matt. editor, *Judaism: History, Belief, and Practice*, New York: Britannica Educational Pub. in association with Rosen Educational Services, 2012.

Stegemann, Ekkehard W. and Stegemann, Wolfgang. *Jesus Movement: A Social History of its First Century*, Fortress, Minneapolis MN (1995, ET 1999).

Steyn, Gert J. "Trajectories of Scripture Transmission: Case of Amos 5:25-27 in Acts 7:42-43," Herv. Teol. Stud, Vol. 69 n.1, Pretoria 1913, 1-7.

Sterling, Gregory. "Opening the Scriptures" in *Jesus and the Heritage of Israel*, edited by David P. Moessner, Trinity, Harrisburg PA, 1999.

Talbert, Charles H. *Reading Acts: Literary and Theological Commentary on the Acts of the Apostles*, Crossroad, NY 1997.

Tannehill, Robert C. *Narrative Unity of Luke—Acts: A Literary Interpretation: Volume Two: Acts of the Apostles*, (Fortress, 1990.

Tarazi, Nadim, Paul. *NT, Luke and Acts*, St. Vladimir's Seminary, Crestwood, NJ, 2001

Taylor, Joan E. *Christians and Holy Places*, Clarendon, New York, 1993.

Thayer, Joseph, Thayer's Greek-English Lexicon of the New Testament, Hendrickson, 1996.

Theissen, Gerd. *Sociology of Early Palestinian Christianity*, Fortress, Phila., 1978.

Topel, L. John. *Children of a Compassionate God: Theological Exegesis of Luke 6:20-49*, Liturgical, Collegeville, MN, 2001.

Tsedaka, Benyamin, ed and trans. *Israelite Samaritan Version of the Torah.* William B. Eerdmans, Grand Rapids, MI 2013.

Tuckett, Christopher. M. *Luke's literary achievement: collected essays*, Sheffield, UK: Sheffield Academic, 1995.

Turner, Henry. *Historicity and Chronology in the New Testament*, London SPCK 1965.

Tyson, Joseph B. *Images in Luke-Acts* University of South Carolina, 1992.

Bibliography

VanderKam, James C. *From Joshua to Caiaphas: High Priests after the Exile*, Fortress, Minneapolis MN, 2004.

———. "Righteous One, Messiah, Chosen One, and Son of Man in 1 Enoch 37-71" in *Messiah: Developments in Earliest Judaism and Christianity*, Minneapolis: Fortress, 1992.

Venter, Pieter M. "The dissolving of marriages in Ezra 9-10 and Nehemiah 13 revisited", *Herv. teol. stud.* vol.74 n.4 Pretoria, 2018, n.p.

Weissenrieder, Annette, *Images of illness in Gospel of Luke: insights of ancient medical texts*, Tübingen: Mohr Siebeck, 2003.

Witherington, Ben, III. *Acts of Apostles, A Socio-Rhetorical Commentary*, Grand Rapids, Eerdmanns 1998.

Wright, Nicholas T. *Acts for Everyone, Part One.* Westminster John Knox, London 2008.

www.ingramcontent.com/pod-product-compliance
Lightning Source LLC
Chambersburg PA
CBHW070455090426
42735CB00012B/2555